ECONOMIC ISSUES, PROBLEMS AND PERSPECTIVES



# U.S.- EU REGULATORY COOPERATION

# Economic Issues, Problems and Perspectives

Additional books in this series can be found on Nova's website under the Series tab.

Additional E-books in this series can be found on Nova's website under the E-book tab.

# Business Economics in a Rapidly-Changing World

Additional books in this series can be found on Nova's website under the Series tab.

Additional E-books in this series can be found on Nova's website under the E-book tab.

ECONOMIC ISSUES, PROBLEMS AND PERSPECTIVES

# U.S.- EU REGULATORY COOPERATION

WILLIAM C. AHRENS
EDITOR

Nova Science Publishers, Inc.
*New York*

For permission to use material from this book please contact us:
Telephone 631-231-7269; Fax 631-231-8175
Web Site: http://www.novapublishers.com



**Library of Congress Cataloging-in-Publication Data**

U.S.--EU regulatory cooperation / editor, William C. Ahrens.
p. cm.
Includes index.
ISBN 978-1-62100-745-6 (softcover)
1. Trade regulation--International cooperation. 2. Trade regulation--United States. 3. Trade regulation--European Union countries. 4. United States--Commerce--European Union countries. 5. European Union countries--Commerce--United States. I. Ahrens, William C. II. Title: United States--European Union regulatory cooperation.
HD3612.U155 2011
382'.3094--dc23

2011038574

*Published by Nova Science Publishers, Inc. † New York*

# CONTENTS

# PREFACE

The United States and the European Union (EU) economic relationship is the largest in the world—and it is growing. The modern U.S.-European economic relationship has evolved since World War II, broadening as the six-member European Community expanded into the present 27-member European Union. The ties have also become more complex and interdependent, covering a growing number and type of trade and financial activities. This book discusses the regulatory cooperation and economic relations between the United States and the European Union.

Chapter 1- Commercial ties between the United States and the 27-member European Union are substantial, growing, and mutually beneficial. However, differences in regulatory approaches limit an even more integrated marketplace from developing. To deal with this situation, a variety of government-to-government efforts have been created to dismantle existing regulatory barriers and to prevent new ones from emerging. These efforts fall under the rubric of transatlantic regulatory cooperation (TRC) and are at the heart of today's U.S.-EU economic relationship.

Chapter 2- The United States and the European Union (EU) share a comprehensive, dynamic, and mutually beneficial economic relationship. Transatlantic markets are among the most open in the world and are deeply integrated. Although the global economic crisis has had a significant negative impact on the transatlantic economy, the great stake each side has had in the other's economy has afforded both sides the ability to withstand the worst of each other's current economic downturn. The key measure of the strength of the transatlantic relationship has been the ability of both sides to work with each other to weather the financial storm.

Chapter 3- The United States and the European Union (EU) economic relationship is the largest in the world—and it is growing. The modern U.S.-European economic relationship has evolved since World War II, broadening as the six-member European Community expanded into the present 27-member European Union. The ties have also become more complex and interdependent, covering a growing number and type of trade and financial activities.

Chapter 4- The 112$^{th}$ Congress, in both its legislative and oversight roles, will confront numerous issues that affect the trade and economic relationship between the United States and the European Union (EU). As U. S. -EU commercial interactions drive significant job creation on both sides of the Atlantic, Congress can be expected to monitor ongoing efforts to deepen transatlantic ties that are already large, dynamic, and mutually beneficial.

U.S. and European private stakeholders, concerned about slow growth, job creation, and increased competition from emerging economies, have urged Brussels and Washington to strengthen transatlantic trade and economic ties by reducing or eliminating remaining trade barriers and by cooperating more closely in addressing global economic challenges. A select group of these issues are examined in this report.

In: U.S.- EU Regulatory Cooperation
Editor: William C. Ahrens

ISBN: 978-1-62100-745-6


*Chapter 1*

# TRANSATLANTIC REGULATORY COOPERATION: BACKGROUND AND ANALYSIS[1]

***Raymond J. Ahearn***

## SUMMARY

Commercial ties between the United States and the 27-member European Union are substantial, growing, and mutually beneficial. However, differences in regulatory approaches limit an even more integrated marketplace from developing. To deal with this situation, a variety of government-to government efforts have been created to dismantle existing regulatory barriers and to prevent new ones from emerging. These efforts fall under the rubric of transatlantic regulatory cooperation (TRC) and are at the heart of today's U.S.-EU economic relationship.

This report is intended to serve as an introduction and primer on a complicated, broad, and often highly technical set of issues. Since the mid-1990s, both U.S. and European multinational companies have viewed

---

[1] [1] This is an edit, reformatted and augmented version of the Congressional Research Service Report for Congress RL34717

divergent ways of regulating markets for both goods and services as the most serious barriers to transatlantic commerce. The primary reason why these companies seek to achieve greater harmonization in standards and regulatory procedures is to reduce costs imposed by having to comply with two different sets of regulations and standards.

TRC must deal with a number of key differences between the United States and EU concerning approaches to regulation. These differences involve political support for regulation and public attitudes towards risk and transparency. Until they converge or are re-aligned, a transatlantic gap in regulatory policies is likely to persist.

Regulatory cooperation is an umbrella concept that incorporates a broad range of activities. At one end of the spectrum are information exchanges and dialogues among regulators that are designed to build trust and confidence. At the other end of the spectrum are activities designed to harmonize regulatory approaches through acceptance of common principles and standards. In between are activities that involve varying degrees of intrusion into the autonomy of regulators.

TRC initiatives have made progress in reducing costs to businesses and consumers in some sectors, but not in others. One of the key obstacles to more extensive cooperation frequently cited is the domestic orientation of regulatory agencies involved in the process. To promote more effective TRC, two policy options are commonly advanced: (1) attracting high-level political support and (2) increasing dramatically the involvement of legislators (Congress and the European Parliament). The Transatlantic Economic Council (TEC), which was created in April 2007, was designed, in part, to generate the kind of high-level political support that previous initiatives may have lacked.

At the last TEC meeting, held in December 2010, the two sides agreed to focus on aligning regulations in emerging technologies, such as nanotechnology or electric cars, before laws or regulations have been promulgated. Previous efforts to harmonize regulations on a sector-by-sector basis proved difficult due to bureaucratic resistance.

TRC has been mostly an executive branch driven process. Yet, through authorization and appropriations of the many different regulatory agencies involved in TRC, Congress could play a more central role if it decided to move in this direction. As domestic regulation takes place in an increasingly integrated transatlantic marketplace, Congress will be called upon to balance the often competing demands of trade expansion and barrier reduction against domestic health and safety concerns.

# INTRODUCTION

The United States and the 27-Member European Union (EU) share a huge, dynamic and mutually beneficial economic partnership.[1] Not only is the U.S.-EU commercial relationship, what many call the transatlantic economy, the largest in the world, it is also arguably the most important.[2] While the transatlantic market is today highly integrated due in large part to a massive amount of foreign direct investment by both U.S. and European companies in each other's markets, differences in regulatory approaches, standards, and philosophies militate against the development of an even tighter and more integrated marketplace. Regulatory differences are also behind some of the most politically sensitive bilateral trade disputes.

To deal with this situation, a variety of government-to-government efforts and transatlantic dialogues have been created to increase understanding between policymakers and regulators on both sides of the Atlantic, to minimize existing regulatory barriers, and to prevent the emergence of new regulatory barriers. These efforts, falling under the rubric of transatlantic regulatory cooperation (TRC), are seen as being important to today's U.S.-EU economic relationship. Proponents maintain that TRC undertakings can not only prevent disruptive and costly trade disputes from occurring, but also spur trade and investment flows by reducing costs for producers and consumers on both sides of the Atlantic.

Since the establishment of the New Transatlantic Agenda (NTA) in 1995, there have been a number of new TRC initiatives, all aimed at removing or reducing regulatory barriers to trade.[3] While each of these initiatives has made some progress towards reducing regulatory burdens, many U.S. and European companies heavily engaged in the transatlantic marketplace maintain that the results have not been materially significant.

At the 2007 U.S.-EU Summit, leaders of the EU and U.S. committed their governments to increasing the efficiency and transparency of transatlantic economic cooperation and to accelerating the reduction and elimination of barriers to international trade and investment with the ultimate objective of achieving a barrier free transatlantic market. They also agreed on a Framework for Advancing Transatlantic Economic Integration (the Framework) and created a new institutional structure, the Transatlantic Economic Council (TEC), to advance the process of regulatory cooperation and barrier reduction. Headed on both sides by ministerial-level appointees, the TEC is designed to oversee the efforts outlined in the Framework, with the goal of accelerating progress and guiding work between the Summits.[4]

Whether the TEC will herald a new era of more effective cooperation remains to be seen. Much could depend upon whether the TEC can exert enough political leverage to convince regulators to make reforms that will result in reduction of regulatory barriers between the EU and the United States, as well as increase the role that legislators on both sides of the Atlantic play in the process. Five TEC meetings have been held since it was established in 2007, the most recent in December 2010 in Washington, D.C.

This report is intended to serve as an introduction and primer on a complicated, broad, and often highly technical set of issues. It is presented in seven parts: the first section describes the nature and scope of U.S.-EU regulatory barriers; the second section explains the rationale for regulatory cooperation; the third section highlights the differences in U.S.-EU regulatory approaches; the fourth section examines the various forms of regulatory cooperation; the fifth section evaluates the results of past initiatives at regulatory cooperation; the sixth section analyzes the creation and operation of the Transatlantic Economic Council; and the last section highlights the role of Congress in transatlantic regulatory cooperation. This report will be updated as events warrant.

## U.S.-EU Regulatory Barriers

Since the mid-1990s, both U.S. and European multinational companies (MNCs) have viewed divergent ways of regulating markets for both goods and services as the most serious barriers to transatlantic commerce. Redundant standards, testing, and certification procedures are seen by these companies as far more costly and harmful than any trade barriers imposed at the border, such as tariffs or quotas. While the purpose of many regulations is to protect consumers and the environment, divergent domestic regulations and standards can affect the competitive position of firms, helping some and disadvantaging others by affecting the importation of products not produced or grown according to those requirements.[5]

To the extent that product standards differ, exporters may find their goods prohibited from certain markets or subject to expensive re-labeling, re-packaging, or re-testing. For example, European winemakers intending to sell in the U.S. market must label their bottles according to U.S. requirements, which are different than EU requirements. Similarly, U.S. exports to the EU of poultry washed with anti-microbial treatments have been blocked for years by different health and safety standards.

Different regulations add to the cost of doing business on both sides of the Atlantic and serve as non-tariff barriers to trade in many different economic activities and sectors. These include but certainly are not limited to differences in accounting and financial reporting requirements, antitrust or competition procedures, consumer protection (safety and health) standards, environmental regulations, and personal data transmission. Each of these divergences can materialize into politically charged disputes and threaten the functioning of the transatlantic market.

In no area has this been a greater problem than in chemicals. In this sector, the U.S. and EU have fundamentally different regulations on issues such as genetically modified organisms (GMOs), hormones, and the registration and restriction of chemical substances. In the case of GMOs, these differences have translated into longer authorization times and stricter standards for approval, release, and marketing of GMOs in the EU than in the U.S. Moreover, GMOs have been the subject of a long and bitter trade dispute brought before the World Trade Organization.[6]

Pharmaceuticals is another sector where regulatory differences have been described as not only significant, but also bewildering. Just in the area of drug approvals, primary regulatory elements governing testing protocols, submission of clinical data, and certification of good manufacturing practices vary considerably between the U.S. and EU. Moreover, within the EU, where public health policy is still a national prerogative, rules and protocols can vary greatly from member state to member state. Because each member state has its own rules and protocols, it can be quite expensive for pharmaceutical companies to achieve marketing authorization throughout the EU or even a subset of countries.[7]

Another example comes from the automotive sector, where American and European car makers sell similar products in the United States and Europe. But there are different standards and testing requirements for all kinds of parts, ranging from headlights, wiper blades, light beams, and seat belts to crash standards—which critics maintain are without measurable differences in safety benefits. There are even multiple crash test dummies of the same or similar size and purpose—a clear example of where regulatory requirements diverge.[8]

Despite the salience of regulatory barriers in transatlantic commerce, a comprehensive, sector-by-sector study or inventory of regulatory barriers has not been undertaken. Proponents argue that such a report could identify regulatory differences that impose substantial burdens on transatlantic commerce and possibilities for their reduction or convergence without compromising either U.S. or EU health and safety priorities. In 2003, the European Commission (EC) proposed that such a study be undertaken and jointly funded, but the U.S. government did not back the initiative. Both sides, however, note the major regulatory divergences that are considered trade barriers in their respective annual trade barrier reports. In the 2008 U.S. trade barriers report, for example, 12 pages are devoted specifically to EU regulatory barriers.[9]

# RATIONALE FOR TRANSATLANTIC REGULATORY COOPERATION

Efforts to enhance TRC draw on both economic and political justifications and are strongly supported by business interests and governments on both sides of the Atlantic. At the same time, within the United States, some interests, mostly academics, see greater benefits derived from regulatory competition and independence, whereby each side is free to maintain its own approach to regulating consumer, health, and environmental issues. The case for non-cooperation or at least caution is also based on concerns that domestic health and safety standards may be compromised by a process that is driven substantially by business interests and stakeholders and could be affected by a "race to the bottom" regarding U.S. and EU standards.

## Economic Rationale

The primary reason why many export industries seek to achieve greater harmonization in international standards is to reduce costs associated with complying with two different sets of regulations and standards. To the extent that transatlantic regulatory standards and procedures differ, the costs of engaging in transatlantic commerce increase.[10]

A good example comes from the auto industry. According to a trade association, a U.S.-based producer of light trucks looked into exporting a model to Europe and found that its design was incompatible with a European regulation on exterior edge projection (the U.S. has no comparable standard). The truck was never exported because it would have required a major and costly redesign. The same truck manufacturer then undertook to ensure that another model on the drawing boards would have maximum export potential built into its design. In order to sell this product in Europe, the manufacturer reportedly utilized 100 unique parts, incurred an additional $42 million in design and developmental costs, and committed an additional 130 people to the program. Yet, the performance of the vehicle, in terms of safety, was unchanged. European-based manufacturers face the same issues in reverse when contemplating selling a European-designed model in the United States. These separate regulations, in turn, may cost manufactures millions of extra dollars to comply with, but may result in no changes in the vehicle in terms of safety or fuel economy.[11]

A 2005 OECD study is often cited to illustrate how costly regulatory barriers to producers and consumers on both sides of the Atlantic. This study estimates that regulatory divergences between the U.S. and Europe costs the United States a sum that is equivalent to 1%-3% of GDP annually.[12]

In addition to cost savings that might be derived from the harmonization of regulations so as to facilitate open markets, it is argued that regulatory cooperation between states will help ensure that regulatory standards will not serve as obstacles to freer trade or unfair trade advantages.[13] Just as internal regulatory divergences can become a source of competitive advantage or trade tension, proponents of regulatory convergence assert that differences in emissions standards, labeling requirements and attitudes towards public health risks between countries can become a market access barrier for foreign products or provide domestic producers with "unfair" competitive advantages.

Proponents of regulatory cooperation maintain that it could have the effect of preventing a welfare-reducing "race to the bottom" as jurisdictions seek to advance the competitiveness of their own industries through lax regulation or lower standards. This rationale for regulatory cooperation served to justify a large expansion of federal legislation and institutions in the United States in the areas of environmental regulation, consumer protection, health and safety, and labor protections. Similar fears of trade distortions and races to the bottom led to the implementation of sweeping harmonization programs and centralized legislation in the EU.[14]

Cast in the context of the global economy, some view TRC as a way for the U.S. and EU to promote global regulatory standards. In the absence of world standards, the U.S. and Europe are often competing for acceptance of their respective regulations in third markets. Proponents of TRC indicate that the net effect of this competition is that India and China can play the United States off against Europe, developing their own technical standards and financial regulations, complicating world trade for everyone.[15]

## Political Rationale

Supporters of TRC note that since the end of the Cold War, the United States and Europe have been searching for various ways to bolster the foundation of the relationship. Absent the common enemy embodied in the threat posed by the former Soviet Union, both sides have felt freer to pursue their own narrow economic and political interests. In the process, trade disputes have appeared to increase in frequency, focusing often on differences in regulation, rather than the traditional barriers of tariffs and subsidies.

To deal with the joint task of giving the relationship a new rationale as well as bolstering overall ties, numerous attempts have been made since the 1995 NTA to enhance transatlantic economic cooperation. In this context, efforts to advance regulatory cooperation have been part of attempts to reinvigorate and upgrade the bilateral relationship. Annual summits, attended by the U.S. President, the President of the European Commission, and the President of the European Council, have been the venue for bringing high-level political attention and focus on efforts to enhance transatlantic regulatory cooperation. Regulatory cooperation, now entailing an expanding group of stakeholders and networks, has become a significant component of the U.S.-EU economic relationship. Supporters argue that through such cooperation the partners may be able to find ways to amicably and expeditiously resolve commercial disputes, as well as establish joint approaches to a number of common regulatory challenges that have global importance.[16]

Because the United States and European Union collectively represent over 50% of global production, in areas where they can agree on a common regulatory policy or approach, they are well-positioned to promote it globally. Where they disagree, there is often deadlock, reflecting the equal size of their economies and markets.[17]

While there are other forums (such as the World Trade Organization and international treaties) to promote regulatory cooperation, they are seen as having shortcomings. The WTO, for example, promotes regulatory cooperation by giving some international standards legal effect, nudging WTO Members to actively participate in international standardization bodies. It also puts national provisions to the test in various committees and offers its members a platform to facilitate regulatory cooperation.[18] But the number of transatlantic regulatory differences that fall within the scope of WTO rules constitute a relatively small proportion of the regulatory policies and procedures that involve firms on both sides of the Atlantic. Moreover, the few regulatory-based trade disputes that the WTO has decided sometimes exacerbate rather than lessen tensions between the US and EU.[19] For this reason, it is argued that the United States and EU need to develop bilateral mechanisms for coordinating their regulatory policies.[20]

### Counter-Arguments

Although there is strong support for TRC among business and government leaders on both sides of the Atlantic, the concept and rationale have their critics. This opposition is based, in part, on an alternative view of the benefits of regulatory competition as opposed to a centrally adopted regulatory framework constructed through regulatory cooperation. These mostly academic critics see benefits in variations in regulatory approaches across jurisdictions (either intra-state or interstate) as a way of disciplining overarching governments and creating incentives for bureaucratic efficiency. They argue that regulatory competition leads to the adoption of standards of varying stringency that efficiently match the needs and desires of each jurisdiction. Because conditions, tastes, and incomes tend to vary across jurisdictions, this school of thought maintains that an optimal regulatory policy for one jurisdiction will not necessarily be optimal for another.

Some consumer groups caution against the influential role that business groups play in transatlantic regulatory cooperation. The concern is that safety and health concerns may be compromised if business groups play such a prominent role in negotiations over testing requirements and standards for their own products. Rather than reducing barriers per se, the Trans Atlantic Consumers Dialogue maintains that the purpose of regulatory cooperation between the United States and EU should be to promote higher health and safety standards, thereby improving consumer welfare on both sides of the Atlantic.[21]

Opponents of TRC assert from this perspective that a great number of centralized regulatory programs should be dismantled and regulatory powers should be decentralized. They believe that regulatory cooperation also reaches its limits where there is lack of institutional architecture to enforce decisions.[22]

## U.S.-EU Differences in Regulatory Approaches

Transatlantic regulatory cooperation must deal with a number of key differences between the United States and EU concerning approaches to regulation. Key differences bear on political cycles affecting regulation, public preferences and tolerance for risk, attitudes towards transparency, and institutional capacities to undertake regulatory reforms. These key differences—whether they pertain to product safety, environmental protection, securities trading, or customs procedures—in how regulations are developed and applied, in turn, raise challenges about whether and how to merge, harmonize, or converge the varied approaches. Until the regulatory structures themselves become more convergent or aligned, the major divergences in regulatory policies are unlikely to disappear.

## Political Cycles

Over the last 50 years, the political cycles of regulatory policy stringency and expansion in the EU and the United States have not moved together. In the process, many important European and American regulations have diverged.[23]

Beginning in the 1960s, many U.S. regulatory standards were likely more comprehensive and stringent than those adopted by the EU and most member states. The U.S. was typically first to identify new consumer and environmental risks and more likely to adopt relatively risk-averse or precautionary standards for dealing with those risks. For example, from the early 1960s through the mid-1980s, American standards for the approval of new pharmaceutical products were more stringent than in any EU member state, and American automobile emission standards were consistently more stringent than those adopted in Europe. The United States also restricted the use of lead in gasoline more rapidly than did Europe and also acted more aggressively to restrict the use of ozone-depleting chemicals.[24]

But over the last 15 years, a number of European standards have become more stringent and comprehensive than U.S. standards.[25] For example, European standards for the approval and labeling of genetically modified (GM) foods and seeds are far more stringent than those adopted by the United States. Recently approved legislation on chemicals (Registration, Evaluation, and Authorization of Chemicals or REACH) has made European standards for the approval of both existing and new chemicals much more demanding than in the U.S. The EU has also moved more aggressively than the United States to impose restrictions on greenhouse gas emissions.

However, in the aftermath of rising concerns about the safety of imported products and the financial crisis caused by the proliferation of sub-prime mortgages, support for more aggressive regulatory actions is rising in the

United States. If the pendulum in the United States swings back towards increased regulation, this may narrow some of the current transatlantic regulatory divergences.[26]

## Values and Public Preferences

Some transatlantic regulatory differences reflect different public preferences and values. For example, many European consumers tend to prefer "naturally produced" foods, while many American consumers are more accepting of products produced by advanced forms of agricultural production. This difference helps to explain, in part, why Europe has imposed restrictions on the use of growth hormones for both beef and dairy cows, while the U.S. has not. It also explains, in part, the relative lack of political controversy in the U.S. surrounding the introduction of biotechnology compared to the more negative response to this technology in Europe.[27]

The United States and EU also operate two different systems of risk management. As in the case of GMOs, the U.S. system is relatively science-based and prefers to regulate once significant problems have been identified. This approach has strong support of farmers, industry, and government officials. On the European side, the public tends to favor a more cautious approach, preferring to regulate out of precaution before a problem has occurred. The food safety scandals of the 1990s increased the resolve of EU member governments to put in place ever more strict regulation for the pre-approval, traceability and labeling of all GMOs, independent of their individual safety characteristics.[28]

## Transparency and Rule-Making

The United States and EU provide for very different degrees of public participation in rule-making. In the United States, Congress passes laws, but generally grants broad authority to the administrative or regulatory agencies to implement those laws through regulations. On occasion, Congress also provides specific direction to these agencies.

Regulations proposed by U.S. administering agencies are subject to considerable public input due in large part to the requirements of the U.S. Administrative Procedures Act (APA), the Freedom of Information Act, and the Government in the Sunshine Act, which permit public scrutiny of regulatory activity. A myriad of laws, executive orders, and bulletins ensure that transparency remains part of the regulatory process. Federal agencies are required to publish in the Federal Register, not just the proposed rule, but the supporting justification for the rule and the entire analytic justification behind it.

EU directives (which serve the same function as U.S. regulations) tend to be developed by the European Commission without as much input from either the public, business or elected officials. The European Parliament, however, has to approve or pass the directives (legislation) proposed by the Commission. While the EU has a number of "better regulation" procedures and guidelines, it has no effective equivalent to the APA.[29]

Recognizing that the United States and EU have become each other's most important stakeholder, both sides may have an interest in ensuring that the other will have the opportunity, method, and forum for participating constructively in each other's regulatory process.

## Institutional Capacity to Undertake Reforms

There also major differences in institutional capacities to undertake regulatory reforms. The EU's institutional framework is well suited to making regulatory changes. In broad terms, the EU has developed as a regulatory state with the European Commission taking a leading role in coordinating European wide regulatory policies in pursuit of building a Single Market. The Commission has ample authority to coordinate cooperation on transatlantic regulatory issues. The regulatory culture within the EU internal market is considered "trade friendly" because EU and national regulators operate with dual missions to promote free trade within the internal market while ensuring public safety. But enforcement is usually left to member states, which often results in a different levels of enforcement and different treatment of European and U.S. companies.[30]

In general, U.S. regulatory agencies have the mandate and funding to focus on domestic regulatory issues and they enjoy a fair amount of independence on policy and implementation matters. However, the United States lacks a clear-cut institutional mechanism to coordinate cooperative efforts. And neither the Commerce Department nor the Office of U.S. Trade Representative (USTR), the lead agencies for U.S. undertakings in the realm of transatlantic regulatory cooperation, have authority to overhaul domestic regulatory policymaking. While Commerce and USTR may bring the heads of U.S. regulatory agencies to the negotiating table, the regulatory agencies are not usually funded nor mandated to engage in TRC activities.[31]

An added structural complication on the U.S. side is the role that states play in regulating activities, particularly professional services. Insurance, banking, private pension fund management, and professional services such as engineering and architecture are all subject to state regulation (and some sectors exclusively).[32]

## FORMS OF TRANSATLANTIC REGULATORY COOPERATION

Regulatory cooperation is an elastic concept that subsumes a broad range of activities. At one end of the spectrum, these activities may include simple discussions and sharing of information between regulators—most often on prospective regulations. At the other end of the spectrum, these activities may involve attempts at harmonizing regulatory approaches through acceptance of common principles and standards. In between are activities that involve varying degrees of intrusion into the autonomy of regulators. One such category is agreements that recognize each other's standards or certification procedures. These agreements are known as MRAs or mutual recognition agreements. The line between each category can be arbitrary and vague, and there are other activities associated with regulatory cooperation that may not fall neatly into one of the above categories.[33]

To date, most efforts at transatlantic regulatory cooperation have been associated with information exchanges and dialogues. Considerable efforts have also been made at negotiating MRAs for a range of goods, as well as other attempts to recognize the adequacy of each others standards in specific areas such as data privacy and accounting. Little has been undertaken in regard to harmonization of standards. What follows is a short elaboration of activities that apply to each of these regulatory activities.

### Information Exchanges and Dialogues

The most basic form of regulatory cooperation involves the establishment of a working group or dialogue for an exchange of information. The group, which may be comprised of technical experts or regulators from different jurisdictions, may meet on an ad hoc and informal basis or may be more structured. A primary objective of these consultations may be to better understand technical differences in standards or regulations and to consult with each other prior to new regulations becoming effective.

Making an effort to work with or consult with each other prior to new regulations becoming effective is viewed as one way to minimize unnecessary regulatory barriers. The exchange of people and information is also expected to build trust and confidence, with the hope of making for more informed and coordinated regulations and may eventually lead to agreement on what constitutes best regulatory practice.

While an exchange of views and a discussion of different issues will not necessarily bring about a meeting of the minds in the technical assessment of a certain field of regulation, it is a necessary first step if convergence is to take place. Where there is no attempt at dialogue, efforts to restrain unilateral legislative actions that could create new regulatory barriers are unlikely to be successful.[34]

In the transatlantic context, a number of U.S. regulatory agencies (e.g., the Securities and Exchange Commission, the Food and Drug Administration, the National Highway Traffic Administration, and the Occupational Safety and Health Administration) have engaged in these kinds of information exchanges and non-binding dialogues with their European counterparts over the past decade. These exchanges were encouraged by the *Guidelines on Regulatory Cooperation and Transparency* which the United States and EU negotiated as part of the 1998 Transatlantic Economic Partnership (TEP). The guidelines were intended to enhance cooperation between EU and US regulators in the development of technical regulations and specifically referred to regular consultation, exchange of data and information, as well as informing one another at an early stage on planned new regulation.

Since 2004, the annual U.S.-EU summits have reinforced efforts at regulatory cooperation. A *Roadmap for Regulatory Cooperation* provides a framework of specific activities in 15 different sectors (e.g., pharmaceuticals, telecommunications equipment, food safety, and auto safety). Subsequent summits have prescribed cooperation for "lighthouse projects" in the fields of intellectual property rights, secure trade, financial markets, innovation and technology, as well as the elimination of obstacles to investment. In addition, a *High Level Regulatory Cooperation Forum,* comprised of regulators from both sides, was established to find common ground on horizontal issues such as risk assessment, cost-benefit analysis and impact analysis when promulgating regulations.

## Mutual Recognition Agreements

A stronger form of cooperation involves MRAs. This cooperation entails an agreement by regulators to accept products or services from another jurisdiction under specified conditions, so that actors complying with the regulations of one jurisdiction will be considered to be in compliance with the rules in another jurisdiction. These kind of agreements can focus on the mutual recognition of conformity assessment certifications or the alignment of relevant standards.

Under full recognition of standards, companies, for example, could sell pharmaceuticals in the United States after meeting European standards without first obtaining FDA approval. An agreement on conformity assessment procedures is a smaller step, requiring domestic regulators to accept the competency of their foreign counterparts to conduct product testing, inspection, or certification. The basic premise behind this kind of MRA is that products could be tested once and considered to have been tested in both markets.[35]

In 1998, the United States and EU completed an MRA for testing and certification requirements covering multiple sectors, including telecommunications and information technology equipment, pharmaceuticals, electronics, electromagnetic compatibility, sports boats and medical devices. The MRA did not provide for mutual recognition of product standards, but it identified certification bodies in the exporting country that could assess the conformity of a range of traded goods with standards of the destination country. The MRAs, thus, introduced competition between assessors or certification bodies.

Competition among certification entities was familiar in Europe, where private firms had long provided certification, but was new in the United States where government agencies had dominated the process. As a result, while some U.S. officials believed that the MRAs would lead to cheaper and more rapid certification, others were concerned about its implications for product safety.[36]

The MRAs did not result in any kind of binding legal agreement between the United States and the EU. Rather they were accomplished through an exchange of letters between the heads of the relevant regulatory agencies. To be implemented successfully, MRAs require that regulators on both sides of the Atlantic have confidence that the other side will not try to attract more business by being deliberately lax. Similarly, regulators need to recognize that each other's safety standards and inspection requirements are basically equivalent.[37]

## Harmonization/Agreement on Regulatory Standards

The strongest form of regulatory cooperation involves harmonization or agreement on the same standards or rules applied across jurisdictions. This could extend not only to regulatory targets (e.g., the permissible level of a particular pollutant in each jurisdiction or reserve requirements among banks), but also to the manner by which regulators ensure compliance with their regulations.

In the transatlantic context, few precedents exist for acceptance or adoption of similar or identical standards. While there have been numerous political declarations calling for regulatory convergence and harmonization, few changes have been enacted in each side's existing laws that would move their regulatory regimes in this direction. The transatlantic market, of course, is not a single market with common institutions pushing for further economic integration. But various stakeholders, frustrated by the slow progress in transatlantic regulatory cooperation, have made proposals that could push the two sides in the direction of adopting a new institutional architecture, such as a binding regulatory cooperation agreement.[38]

Those who see a binding treaty or regulatory cooperation agreement as necessary institutional architecture to achieve a transatlantic single market point to EU integration as a model. In moving towards the completion of a Single European Market, the Commission issued a white paper that listed the pieces of legislation requiring harmonization, and simultaneously identified the institutional mechanisms to achieve specified ends.[39]

U.S. public support for such an approach could depend on whether the goal of such a treaty or legal agreement was the development of identical legislation or comparable legislation. If the goal was identical legislation, much resistance to this kind of deeper integration could be expected from a number of quarters. This is particularly true from stakeholders who view movement in this direction as leading to a loss of regulatory autonomy for U.S. authorities. If the goal was the development of similar or comparable legislation that facilitates mutual recognition, much less resistance perhaps could be expected.[40]

# RESULTS OF PAST INITIATIVES AT REGULATORY COOPERATION

The United States and EU have pursued a variety of policy initiatives and new mechanisms over the past 15 years to reduce or eliminate regulatory barriers. The results have been mixed. A number of these initiatives have been successful in some regulatory areas, while transatlantic regulatory cooperation has not made material differences for businesses or consumers in some other sectors. Assuming it is concluded that stronger regulatory cooperation is desirable, an assessment of past efforts could be useful.

## Highlights of Past Initiatives

Beginning in 1990 with the Transatlantic Declaration, regular U.S.-EU summits were initiated to reinvigorate and upgrade the bilateral relationship. Attended by the U.S. President, the President of the European Commission, and the President of the European Council, the summits were intended to bring high-level focus to cooperative activities. Successive summits have led to a number of agreements relating to transatlantic regulatory cooperation:

- At the 1995 summit in Madrid, the United States and EU formally adopted the New Transatlantic Agenda (NTA) in an effort to provide a new foundation for the partnership. The NTA was accompanied by a detailed action plan. In addition, the NTA set up a comprehensive and regular government-to-government dialogue, as well as four dialogues between stakeholders on both sides of the Atlantic. These included the Transatlantic Business Dialogue (TABD), the Transatlantic Labor Dialogue (TALD), the Transatlantic Environmental Dialogue (TAED) and the Transatlantic Consumer Dialogue (TACD).
- Pursuant to the NTA, the two sides focused particular attention on problems posed by divergent standards and certification systems. In addition to promoting the convergence in regulatory systems, efforts were undertaken to negotiate MRAs covering several sectors. In 1998, MRAs affecting sectors such as electrical equipment, pharmaceutical products, telecommunications and information technology equipment were reached.

- At the 1998 summit in London, the Transatlantic Economic Partnership (TEP) was created to improve bilateral economic and trade relations and to help create a more open world trading system. The TEP established deadlines for particular actions within the areas of regulatory cooperation, mutual recognition, and consumer product safety.
- At the Bonn Summit in June 1999, a Joint Statement on *Early Warning and Problem Prevention Mechanisms* was adopted. The warning system was designed to identify regulations, preferably still in draft form, that might contribute to non-tariff barriers to trade.
- At the 2000 U.S.-EU Summit in Lisbon, the Consultative Forum on Biotechnology was established to improve communication and understanding on the various concerns involved in biotechnology.
- At the May 2002 summit in Washington, the two sides reached agreements on *Guidelines for Regulatory Cooperation and Transparency*. These sought to take the idea of an early warning system a step further by encouraging U.S. and EU regulatory agencies to consult on a voluntary basis, sharing work plans that identify areas of anticipated regulatory action for the coming year and offering opportunities for reaction before regulations are finalized.[41]
- Moving towards a more systematic cooperative approach, a *Roadmap for EU-U.S. Regulatory Cooperation and Transparency* was developed in June 2004. It listed 10 specific projects for regulatory discussion and also expanded the approach to horizontal initiatives.
- The 2005 EU-U.S. Summit produced a second *Roadmap for EU-U.S. Regulatory Cooperation and Transparency* and expanded the list to 15 sector-specific projects. It also established two new dialogues. One was between the European Commission and Office of Management and Budget on transparency and methodologies for impact and risk assessment, in order to improve understanding of each other's regulatory systems. A second, a *High-Level Regulatory Cooperation Forum*, was tasked to develop a joint regulatory work plan based on mutual best practices. Its members include senior U.S. and European Commission officials, academics, business executives, and other officials.

## Accomplishments

Among the accomplishments are the following.

1. Most observers would agree that new mechanisms for dialogue and information exchange have improved mutual understanding and day-to-day working relationships among economic regulators in a wide range of sectors; Arguably, cooperation is now far deeper, broader, more decentralized and routine than it had been before in areas such as pharmaceuticals, medical devices, financial services and marine equipment.
2. The NTA process and related efforts at regulatory cooperation fostered closer relationships among many stakeholders, including business people representing the major corporations investing in both Europe and the United States. In particular, the TABD, representing a transatlantic coalition of big businesses on both sides of the Atlantic, developed into an "effective framework for enhanced cooperation between the transatlantic business community and the governments of the European Union and the United States."[42]
3. The NTA and subsequent summits enhanced on-going efforts to increase the compatibility of U.S. and EU approaches to competition policy. According to one observer, much convergence in substantive standards has been achieved voluntarily through the exchange of ideas and institutional learning processes.[43]
4. MRAs (discussed previously) covering over $50 billion in trade were implemented in three sectors, leading to significant cost savings for U.S. businesses; several of the agreements provided for U.S. and EU testing facilities to recognize each other's standards over time, thus allowing firms to have products tested only once on either side of the Atlantic. The Commerce Department estimated that the agreement would save U.S. industries more than $1 billion in testing and certification costs.[44]
5. The 2002 *Guidelines for Regulatory Cooperation* promoted a number of procedural steps that most likely have facilitated a more effective dialogue. These steps included arrangements to permit sharing of non-

public information between regulators. The *Roadmap for Regulatory Cooperation* now provides a framework for consultations and dialogue in fifteen different sectors (e.g., pharmaceuticals, telecommunications equipment, food safety and auto safety) with a focus on prospective regulations and reducing regulatory barriers.

6. The U.S.-EU Safe Harbor Agreement was implemented in 2002. This agreement provided an innovative mechanism whereby U.S. firms could be certified as meeting the EU's more demanding data privacy requirements for exporting personal data.
7. In February 2004, the U.S. and EU signed an MRA on marine safety equipment covering $150 million to $200 million annually in two-way trade.[45]
8. The *U.S.-EU High Level Regulatory Cooperation Forum,* established in 2005, has focused on methodologies for generating good regulatory practices. To the extent both sides are able to develop a methodological framework that ensures the comparability of regulatory reviews, with an emphasis on risk assessments, cost/benefit analysis, and trade and investment impacts, unilateral legislative initiatives and the creation of new regulatory barriers can be curtailed.
9. By 2006 the Financial Markets Regulatory Dialogue had reported some progress on recognizing each others' financial standards in specific areas.[46] In particular, progress has been made on gaining the mutual acceptance by 2009 of the equilevance of accounting standards—that is the U.S. Generally Accepted Accounting Principles (GAAP) and International Financial Reporting Standards (IFRS). This will make it easier for European companies to raise capital in the United States and for U.S. companies to raise capital in Europe.[47]

## Disappointments

Specific disappointments include the following.

1. Enthusiasm for mutual recognition as a regulatory strategy faded when three of the six agreements failed to become operational by established deadlines.[48] In the view of some analysts, these MRAs were never implemented due to the U.S. reluctance to recognize the equivalency of European certifiers. In the pharmaceutical and medical device sectors, for example, the FDA had continuing doubts about the

capability of some EU member states to oversee high pharmaceutical standards in laboratories. In the electrical equipment sector, OSHA refused to cede its right to designate which laboratories in Europe could evaluate and certify new electrical products for sale in the United States.[49] A related obstacle on the European side was the EU inclination to regulate at the European level, only to leave enforcement to Member States, which often results in different levels of enforcement and different treatment of European and U.S. companies.[50]

2. Irrespective of annual summits, the TEP, by some accounts, went into hibernation from 1998 to 2004. Despite the many recommendations and political declarations issued during this time period, there were few material accomplishments.[51]
3. Pieces of legislation adopted unilaterally by both sides in 2002 served to put a break on regulatory cooperation by violating the *2002 Guidelines on Regulatory Cooperation* and the *"Early Warning System."* On the one side, the EU imposed its views on how to regulate chemicals by adopting legislation known as REACH, which affected the testing and approval of chemicals, without much input from U.S. stakeholders. On the other side, the United States adopted legislation (Sarbanes-Oxley), which reformed public accounting standards, without taking into account EU views. Both pieces of legislation created considerable difficulties for transatlantic businesses, from companies attempting to raise capital to firms that manufacture everyday goods.
4. Despite extensive efforts at cooperation for nearly two decades, the transatlantic regulatory divide remains large in the area of chemicals. The two sides still maintain fundamentally different regulations on issues such as hormones, genetically modified organisms (GMOs), cosmetics, and the registration and restriction of chemical substances. U.S. and EU regulators continue to operate with starkly different regulatory philosophies and styles. And the record of transatlantic regulatory cooperation in this sphere has been highly contentious, prompting the United States to file a legal complaint with the WTO.[52]
5. There has been lack of material progress in many other sectors, such as autos, and pharmaceuticals. Moreover, past TRC initiatives have tended to be fragmented, poorly coordinated, and lacking in political accountability for success and failure.[53]

## Obstacles and Options for More Extensive Cooperation

In evaluating the history of past initiatives, a number of observers have pointed to several key obstacles to more effective regulatory cooperation. High on this list are the independence of regulatory agencies involved, the lack of committed resources for transatlantic regulatory collaboration, and the sheer complexity of the undertaking. To promote more effective TRC by overcoming these obstacles, three policy options are often put forth: (1) attracting high-level political support for TRC; (2) increasing dramatically the involvement of legislators on both sides in the process; and (3) developing an institutional architecture that can prioritize the problems and challenges that need to be addressed.

Regulatory cooperation, particularly mutual recognition, requires domestic regulators to accept the competency of their foreign counterparts to conduct product testing. A key obstacle, however, is that regulators remain accountable to domestic legislators for the product standards that are applied both to domestic and foreign products. As a result, regulators on both sides of the Atlantic are generally reluctant to transfer authority to a foreign body, and the MRA negotiations demonstrated that some regulatory bodies are more reluctant than others.[54]

Based on the premise that enhanced regulatory cooperation, particularly through mutual recognition, will never happen if matters are left to individual regulatory agencies, high-level political pressure is commonly prescribed. Such pressure, either from the White House, the Congress, or both, may be employed to convince regulators to adopt reforms that result in a reduction of barriers between the United States and EU and/or to make greater efforts to accommodate transatlantic interests when promulgating new regulations.

Successful regulatory cooperation also requires resources for the necessary meetings and dialogues to take place. At least on the U.S. side, the regulatory agencies have no dedicated budgets to support these activities. Accordingly, some stakeholders, such as the U.S. Chamber of Commerce, have proposed that Congress consider the creation of specifically funded mandates to enable U.S. agencies better participate in these transatlantic dialogues.

The scope of the transatlantic regulatory agenda is also extremely broad and technical. Encompassing most regulatory agencies, ranging from the Food and Drug Administration (FDA) and the Consumer Product Safety Commission (CPSC) to the National Highway Traffic Safety Administration (NHTSA) and the Environmental Protection Agency (EPA), and diverse sectors, ranging from pharmaceuticals and cosmetics to telecommunications and marine safety, the status of the agenda at any one time is not easy to ascertain. To move issues forward that are by their nature abstract and technical, some observers have called for creation of a institution that is capable of setting priorities and deciding on which issues are ripe for resolution with the help of higher-level political intervention.

## THE TRANSATLANTIC ECONOMIC COUNCIL

Predicated on the notion that past initiatives failed to make significant progress in enhancing regulatory progress, the Transatlantic Economic Council (TEC) was established in April 2007 at the U.S.-EU Summit as a key component of the *Framework for Advancing Transatlantic Economic Integration.* Created as a new entity by German Chancellor Angela Merkel (then EU Council President), European Commission President Barroso, and President Bush, the TEC is designed to provide minister-level political guidance for implementation of a work program as outlined by the *Framework* to foster regulatory cooperation and to reduce or eliminate regulatory burdens to trade. The Summit leaders also created an advisory group to the TEC and invited the U.S. Congress, along with the European Parliament, to accept a new, more substantive role in transatlantic regulatory cooperation by becoming part of an advisory group. In short, the TEC and the *Framework* are designed to deal with some of the suggested shortcomings (described above) of previous transatlantic regulatory initiatives: lack of high level political leadership and not enough involvement of legislators and other stakeholders in the regulatory process.

The TEC consists of two co-chairs (ministerial-level appointees with cabinet rank) from each side, as well as a number of EU Commissioners and U.S. Cabinet Members for the broad-ranging policy areas covered in the *Framework.* Permanent members of the TEC include the Secretaries of the Treasury and Commerce and the U.S. Trade Representative and the European Commissioners for External Relations, for Trade and Internal Market and Services. In addition, other U.S. Cabinet Members and European Commissioners may participate when the agenda covers issues falling under their jurisdiction.[55]

Given that the two TEC leaders are cabinet-level appointees, the TEC was expected to have the kind of high-level political support that previous efforts at economic integration may have lacked. Such clout, it is argued, may be needed to persuade domestic regulators to yield some of their authorities or to better cooperate with their counterparts across the Atlantic in harmonizing regulatory approaches.[56]

TEC efforts to foster cooperation and reduce regulatory barriers focus on two main types of issues: (1) differences in regulatory processes and approaches; and (2) sectoral or bilateral barriers and disputes. The goal in the first issue area is to find ways to reduce barriers to transatlantic economic integration posed by new regulations and or prevent them from happening. The primary avenue for accomplishing this objective entails efforts to reform, harmonize or converge regulatory processes, both through the development of comparable methodologies to assess risk and do cost-benefit analysis and intensified interactions among regulators. How regulations are developed and applied can have a large impact on the how companies do business not only in the transatlantic marketplace, but in third markets as well.

The goal in the second issue area is to reduce barriers to transatlantic integration caused by regulations in specific sectors. This is to be accomplished by intensified sector-by-sector cooperation, including the promotion of the 2002 U.S.-EU Guidelines for Regulatory Cooperation and case-by-case examination of specific projects called for by the Roadmap for Regulatory Cooperation.[57]

In the first three years (2007-2009) of its four-year history, the TEC was used primarily as a mechanism to try to resolve a number of longstanding bilateral trade disputes, most notably the EU's ban on imports of chlorine-washed poultry. Efforts to harmonize regulations on a sector-by-sector basis also proved difficult due to political and bureaucratic resistance on both sides to revise existing laws and regulations. In late 2010, the two sides agreed to focus future efforts on aligning regulations and standards in emerging or new technologies, (such as nanotechnology or electric cars) well before laws or regulations have been promulgated. Accordingly, at their fifth and most recent meeting, held in Washington on December 17, 2010, the TEC agreed to a work program focusing on sectors where regulatory cooperation can help preclude unintended trade barriers.

Among the highlights of this latest TEC meeting, the two sides agreed to develop a process to implement compatible approaches for the regulation of new and innovative sectors, with the hope of avoiding trade disputes due to different regulations. The meeting also provided new impetus for regulatory cooperation in specific sectors such as electronic health records, energy-saving products, and electric vehicles, as a way of reducing costs and preempting unnecessary obstacles to exports. Finally, the TEC meeting launched an

Innovation Action Plan designed to strengthen joint efforts to promote innovation and the commercialization of emerging technologies.[58]

These work plans were touted by senior officials as more specific and time-bound than previous work plans. Whether the results will be more tangible and commercially significant remains to be seen. Part of the problem is that regulatory cooperation is difficult and technically demanding work, with wide differences between the two sides concerning approaches to regulation. Key differences bear on public preferences and tolerance for risk, attitudes towards transparency, and institutional capacities to undertake regulatory reforms.[59]

# ROLE OF CONGRESS[60]

Since it began nearly two decades ago, transatlantic regulatory cooperation has been for the most part a wholly run undertaking between the executive branches and independent regulatory agencies on both sides of the Atlantic. By and large, TRC exchanges and dialogues have been confined to regulators and officials of the executive branches on both sides of the Atlantic. The *Guidelines on Regulatory Cooperation and Transparency*, in fact, do not apply to Congress or the European Parliament.

The role of Congress in transatlantic regulatory cooperation in the past has been limited mostly to oversight hearings (see Appendix A for a listing) and the introduction of a few resolutions.[61] But Congress has on occasion taken actions that have both thwarted and facilitated regulatory cooperation. For example, on the one hand, some Members of Congress became concerned in the late 1990s that the MRAs the administration was negotiating could harm consumers and undermine health and safety standards. As Representative Henry Waxman (D-CA) put it, "there is no question that international agreements of this kind can enhance the efficiency of commerce, but it is equally clear that they can potentially depress American health and safety standards." According to one observer, such concerns made some U.S. regulators reluctant to participate in the MRA negotiations.[62]

On the other hand, Congress also passed legislation directing the FDA to support efforts of the Department of Commerce and USTR to implement MRAs. In the Food and Drug Administration Modernization Act of 1997 (P.L. 105-115), a bill to speed the FDA approval process for new drugs and medical devices, a provision directed the FDA to support the efforts of Commerce and the Office of the U.S. Trade Representative to implement MRAs. According to the same observer, inclusion of the MRA language in the legislation was an important step toward finishing the agreement.[63]

These examples highlight a larger and more pivotal role Congress could play in regulatory cooperation if it chose to become more involved. To the extent that an overwhelming domestic orientation of regulatory agencies is a problem in moving TRC initiatives forward, Congress has the power through both the authorization and appropriations process to mandate that U.S. regulators cooperate. Congress can also ensure that the U.S. agencies involved in regulatory cooperation have the necessary budgetary and organizational resources to get the job done. Conversely, if Congress views transatlantic initiatives as moving too far in the direction of trade expansion at the expense of safety and health concerns or other priorities, Congress can make it difficult for U.S. agencies to continue on that course of action.

Beyond providing guidance to U.S. regulatory agencies on TRC initiatives, Congress also could play a bigger role in preventing new legislation from causing new transatlantic regulatory barriers. Currently, taking the transatlantic impact (trade and investment effects) into account is not considered in any structured or formal fashion during the legislative process. Yet, political declarations from past U.S.-EU summits backed by the transatlantic business community, have urged a more institutionalized process for making Congress more aware of the potential impact of new legislation on transatlantic trade.

How this could be done is the subject of considerable speculation. One of the factors that has to be considered is the wide range of congressional committees that have primary jurisdiction over issues that are high on the agenda of TRC. As shown in Appendix B, many different authorizing committees have primary jurisdiction over some of the main regulatory agencies involved in TRC activities. On the House side, the Energy and Commerce, Transportation, Judiciary, and Agriculture Committees all have important oversight roles. Counterpart committees on the Senate side include Commerce, Science, and Transportation, Health Education, Labor, and Pensions, Energy and Natural Resources, Environment and Public Works, and Agriculture. Notably absent from this list are the committees charged with overall responsibility for oversight of transatlantic relations, the Senate Foreign Relations and the House Foreign Affairs Committees, and the committees that have primary jurisdiction over trade and investment issues, Senate Finance and the House Ways and Means.

Currently, the only formal institutional link between Congress and transatlantic regulatory cooperation is through the Transatlantic Legislators Dialogue (TLD), an inter-parliamentary exchange between selected Members of the House of Representatives and the European Parliament. The TLD serves as an advisor to the TEC, but its membership and function have raised questions concerning how well it can carry out its role as an advisor to the TEC.[64]

Much of this begs the question whether Congress should be an advisor or a participant in the TRC process, including the annual U.S.-EU Summits. While a more proactive role for Congress would likely enhance the political basis of support for transatlantic regulatory cooperation, it is by no means certain that there is a consensus in favor of developing the necessary mechanisms and mandate to move in this direction.

## APPENDIX A. CONGRESSIONAL HEARINGS ON TRANSATLANTIC REGULATORY COOPERATION

House Committee on Commerce. *Imported Drugs: U.S.-EU Mutual Recognition Agreement on Drug Prescriptions*. October 2, 1998, 32p.

House Committee on Commerce. *The EU Data Protection Directive: Implications for the U.S. Privacy Debate.* March 8, 2001, 48p.

House Committee on Financial Services. *The EU's Financial Services Action Plan and Its Implications for the American Financial Services Industry*. May 22, 2002, 122p.

House Committee on Financial Services. *U.S.-EU Regulatory Dialogue and Its Future.* May 13, 2004, 106p.

House Committee on Financial Services. *U.S.-EU Regulatory Dialogue: The Private Sector Perspective.* June 17, 2004, 79p.

House Committee on Financial Services. *U.S.-EU Economic Relationship: What Comes Next?* June 16, 2005, 86p.

House Committee on International Relations. *Transatlantic Trade Agenda: Conflict or Cooperation?* September 29, 1999.

House Committee on International Relations. *Recognizing the Continued Importance of the Transatlantic Relationship and Promoting Stronger Relations with Europe by Reaffirming the Need for a Continued and Meaningful Dialogue Between the U.S. and Europe*. October 29, 2003, 16p.

Senate Committee on Foreign Relations. *U.S.-EU Cooperation on Regulatory Affairs*. October 16, 2003, 55p.

Senate Committee on Foreign Relations. *U.S.-EU Regulatory Cooperation on Emerging Technologies*, May 11, 2005, 62p.

## Appendix B. U.S.-EU Regulatory Cooperation by Sector, U.S. Regulatory Agency, and Committee Oversight

| Sector[a] | U.S. Regulatory Agency[b] | Committees[c] |
|---|---|---|
| Pharmaceuticals | Food and Drug Administration (FDA) | House: Energy and Commerce; Senate: Health, Education, Labor, and Pensions and Commerce Science and Transportation |
| Automobile Safety | National Highway Traffic Safety Administration (NHTSA) | House: Energy and Commerce; Senate: Commerce, Science and Transportation |
| Information and Communications Standards in Regulations | Department of Commerce, National Institute of Standards and Technology (NIST) | House: Energy and Commerce; Senate: Commerce, Science and Transportation |
| Cosmetics | FDA | House: Energy and Commerce; Senate: Health, Education, Labor, and Pensions |
| Consumer Product Safety | Consumer Product Safety Commission (CPSC) | House: Energy and Commerce; Senate: Commerce, Science, and Transportation |
| Consumer Protection Enforcement Cooperation | Federal Trade Commission (FTC) | House: Energy and Commerce, and Judiciary; Senate: Commerce, Science and Transportation, and Judiciary |
| Unfair Commercial Practices | FTC | House: Energy and Commerce, and Judiciary; Senate: Commerce, Science, and Transportation, and Judiciary |
| Nutritional Labeling | FDA | House: Energy and Commerce, and Agriculture; Senate: Heath, Education, Labor and Pensions, and Agriculture |
| Food Safety | FDA | House: Energy and Commerce Agriculture; Senate: Commerce, Science, and Transportation, and Agriculture |

| **Sector**[a] | **U.S. Regulatory Agency**[b] | **Committees**[c] |
|---|---|---|
| Marine Equipment | U.S. Coast Guard | House: Transportation and Infrastructure; Senate: Commerce, Science, and Transportation |
| Eco-Design | Environmental Protection Agency (EPA); Department of Energy Office of Efficiency and Renewable Energy | House: Energy and Commerce and Science; Senate: Energy and Natural Resources |
| Chemicals | Environmental Protection Agency | House: Energy and Commerce; Senate: Environment and Public Works |
| Energy Efficiency | EPA and Department of Energy | House: Energy and Commerce Senate: Energy and Natural Resources |
| Medical Devices | FDA | House: Energy and Commerce; Senate: |
| Telecommunication s and Radio Communications Equipment | Federal Communications Commission and Department of Commerce, National Institute of Standards and Technology | House: Energy and Commerce; Senate: Commerce, Science, and Transportation |

Source: CRS.

a. These sectors are identified in the 2005 *Roadmap for Regulatory Cooperation*, http:// www.ustr.gov?World_Regions/Europe_Middle_East/Europe/US_EU-Regulatory-C.

b. These agencies are also identified in the 2005 *Roadmap for Regulatory Cooperation*.

c. Depending on the focus of each sectoral initiative, other committees could also have oversight responsibilities. Regarding appropriations, the appropriations subcommittees would tend to vary as well. For example, the House and Senate Appropriations subcommittees on agriculture have jurisdiction over FDA's appropriations. This arrangement reflects, in part, the agency's origin within the Department of Agriculture as the Bureau of Chemistry in 1862

## End Notes

1 For background on the European Union, see CRS Report RS21372, *The European Union: Questions and Answers*, by Kristin Archick and Derek E. Mix.

2 For background on EU-U.S. commercial ties, see CRS Report RL30608, *EU-U.S. Economic Ties: Framework, Scope, and Magnitude*, by William H. Cooper; and CRS Report R41652, *U.S.-EU Trade and Economic Relations: Key Policy Issues for the 112th Congress*, by Raymond J. Ahearn.

3 The NTA committed the United States and EU to work together to achieve four major goals, including the expansion of world trade and closer economic relations. Implementation of the agenda is guided by a joint EU-U.S. Action Plan which is coordinated by a group of senior level officials.

[4] For background on the 2007 U.S.-EU Summit and the TEC, see *http://www.whitehouse.gov/in* focus/ eusummit/2007/.

[5] Daniel C. Esty, "Regulatory Competition in Focus," *Journal of International Economic Law* (2000), pp. 215-217.

[6] Reinhard Quick, "Transatlantic Regulatory Cooperation on Chemicals—An Idealist's Dream?," German Marshall Fund Academic Research Conference, Ford School, University of Michigan. Available at http://www.fordschool.umich.edu/news/events_details/ re_coop_ and-comp_08/, and Gregory C. Shaffer and Mark A. Pollack, "Reconciling Regulatory Differences: The Ongoing Transatlantic Dispute over the Regulation of Biotechnology," in *The Future of Transatlantic Economic Relations,* edited by David M. Andrews, Mark A. Pollack, Gregory C. Shaffer, and Helen Wallace, Robert Schuman Centre for Advanced Studies, 2005, pp. 220-221.

[7] Keith Maskus and Yin He, "Trans-Atlantic Regulatory Cooperation in Pharmaceuticals: An Intellectual Property and Trade Perspective," German Marshall Fund Academic Policy Research Conference, May 8-9, 2008, Ford School, University of Michigan, p. 8. Available at http://www.fordschool.umich.edu/news/events_details/ reg_coop_and_comp_08/.

[8] Vann H. Wilber and Paul T. Eichbrecht, "Transatlantic Trade, the Automotive Sector: The Role of Regulation in a Global Industry, Where We Have Been and Where We Need To Go, How Far Can EU-US Cooperation Go Toward Achieving Regulatory Harmonization," German Marshall Fund Academic Policy Research Conference, Ford School, University of Michigan, p. 7. Available at http://fordschool.umich.edu/news/events_details/re_coop_and _comp_08/.

[9] Office of the U.S. Trade Representative, 2008 National Trade Estimate Report on Foreign Trade Barriers, pp. 9-21. Available at http://www.ustr.gov.

[10] David Vogel, "Can it be done? Suggestions for better regulatory cooperation between the US and Europe," Transatlantic Thinkers #7, BertelsmannStiftung, p. 3. Available at http://www.bertelsmann-stiftung.de/cps/rde/xchg/ bst_engl/hs.xsl/prj_7072-7084.htm.

[11] Vann H. Wilber and Paul T. Eichbrecht, "Transatlantic Trade, the Automotive Sector: The Role of Regulation in a Global Industry, Where We Have Been and Where We Need To Go, How Far Can EU-US Cooperation Go Toward Achieving Regulatory Harmonization," German Marshall Fund Academic Policy Research Conference, May 8-9, 2008, p. 5. Available at http://fordschool.umich.edu/news/events_details/re_coop_andcomp_08/.

[12] OECD Working Paper No. 432, *On the Benefits of Liberalizing Product Markets and Reducing Barriers to International Trade and Investment: The Case of the United States and European Union* May 26, 2005.

[13] The initial impetus for promoting a transatlantic dialogue on regulatory standards was the European Community's 1992 internal market program. At the heart of this program was an effort to establish European-wide standards. Progress along these lines raised concerns in the U.S. business community that the new standards and regulations could be used to disadvantage U.S. exporters and products.

[14] Daniel C. Esty and Damien Geradin, "Regulatory Co-opetition," *Journal of International Economic Law* (2000), 235-255, p. 236.

[15] Transatlantic Policy Network (TPN), *Completing the Transatlantic Market,* February 2007, pp. 6-7. Available at http://tpnonline.org.

[16] Simon J. Everett and Robert M. Stern, "Condemned To Cooperate?," German Marshall Fund Academic Policy Research Conference, May 8-9, 2008, University of Michigan, p. 7. Available at http://www.fordschool.umich.edu/ news/events_details/re_coop_08/.

[17] Gregory Shaffer and Mark Pollack, "How Hard and Soft Law Interact in International Regulatory Governance: Alternatives, Complements or Antagonists?," German Marshall Fund Academic Policy Research Conference, May 8-9, 2008. University of Michigan, p. 5. Available at http://www.fordschool.umich.edu/news/events_details/reg_coop_and comp _08.

[18] Reinhard Quick, "Regulatory Cooperation—A Subject of Bilateral Trade Negotiations or Even for the WTO?," *Journal of World Trade Law* 42(3), 2008, p. 405.

[19] David Vogel, op. cit., p. 4.

[20] Ibid., p. 5.

[21] Trans Atlantic Consumer Dialogue, "Position Paper and Resolution on Horizontal Regulatory Initiatives in EU-U.S. Regulatory Cooperation," February 2007. Available at http://www.tacd.org/cgi-bin/db.cgi?page=view&config=admin/ docs.cfg&id=322.

[22] Reinhard Quick, op. cit., p. 401.

[23] David Vogel, op. cit., p. 14.

[24] Ibid., p. 7.

[25] At the same time, in 1980s and throughout much of the 1990s, much of U.S. policy was driven by efforts to reduce the costs of protective regulations on American companies and, thus, improve the performance of the American economy.

[26] Jackie Calmes, "Both Sides of the Aisle See More Regulation," *New York Times,* October 14, 2008, p. 1.

[27] David Vogel, op. cit., p. 6.

[28] Gregory C. Shaffer and Mark A. Pollack, op. cit., p. 221.

[29] Testimony of Gerard Depayre, Deputy Head of Delegation, European Commission to the United States, "U.S.-EU Cooperation on Regulatory Affairs," Hearing Before the Subcommittee on European Affairs of the Committee on Foreign Relations, U.S. Senate, 108th Congress, 1st session, October 16, 2003, p. 20.

[30] Kalypso Nicolaidis and Rebecca Steffenson, "Managed Mutual Recognition in the Trans-atlantic Marketplace," in *The Future of Transatlantic Economic Relations,* p. 147.

[31] Maria Green Cowles, "Calming the Waters: The Rebirth of the Transatlantic Business Dialogue," in *The Future of Transatlantic Economic Relations,* p. 285.

[32] Kalypso Nicolaidis and Rebecca Steffenson, p. 152.

[33] Alan O. Sykes, "Regulatory Competition or Regulatory Harmonisation? A Silly Question?," *Journal of International Economic Law* (2000), pp. 257-264.

[34] Reinhard Quick, "Regulatory Cooperation," op. cit., p. 402.

[35] Testimony of Stuart Eizenstat, European-American Business Council, Hearing on U.S.-EU Cooperation on Regulatory Affairs, Subcommittee on European Affairs of the Committee on Foreign Relations, U.S. Senate, 108th Congress, 1st session, October 16, 2003, p. 29.

[36] Charan Devereaux, Robert Z. Lawrence, and Michael D. Watkins, "The U.S.-EU Mutual Recognition Agreements," in *Case Studies in US Trade Negotiations,* in Making the Rules, Vol. 1, Institute for International Economics, 2006, p. 304.

[37] Stuart Eisenstadt, op. cit., p. 24.

[38] The U.S. Chamber of Commerce, for example, has proposed an Agreement on Regulatory Cooperation (ARC), a legally binding regulatory cooperation agreement that would oblige both sides to operate under a common set of regulatory principles and core beliefs. The ARC would require regulators to assess the cost impact of forthcoming regulations on transatlantic commerce, adopt other's best practices where possible, and utilize a similar methodology to assess costs and benefits of proposed regulations. See Chamber of Commerce of the United States, Correspondence to U.S. Office of Management and Budget and to the Secretariat General, European Commission, February 8, 2008.

[39] Reinhard Quick, "Regulatory Cooperation," p. 401.

[40] Ibid.

[41] The Atlantic Council of the United States, *Risk and Reward: U.S.-EU Regulatory Cooperation on Food Safety and the Environment,* Policy Paper, November 2002, p. 7.

[42] Maria Green Cowles, "Calming the Waters: The Rebirth of the Transatlantic Business Dialogue," p. 278.

[43] Robert Anderson, "Competition (Antitrust) Policy: What Balance of Cooperation and Regulation in the Transatlantic Sphere?," German Marshall Fund Academic Policy

Research Conference, May 8-9, 2008, Ford School, University of Michigan, p. 5. Available at http://www.fordschool.umich.edu/news/events_details/reg_coop_and_comp_08/.

[44] Maria Green Cowles, "Calming the Waters: The Rebirth of the Transatlantic Business Dialogue," p. 280.

[45] Charon Devereaux, Robert Z. Lawrence, and Michael D. Watkins, "The U.S.-EU Mutual Recognition Agreements," p. 348.

[46] Elliott Posner, "Market Power without a Single Market: The New Transatlantic Relations in Financial Services," In *The Future of Transatlantic Economic Relations: Continuity Amid Discord,* July 2005.

[47] Andreas Noelke, Johan Wolfgang Goethe Universitat, "Transatlantic Regulatory Cooperation on Accounting Standards: A 'Varieties of Capitalism' Perspective," German Marshall Fund Academic Policy Research Conference, May 8-9, 2008, Ford School, University of Michigan. Available at http://fordschool.umich.edu/news/events_details_/reg_cop_and_comp_08/.

[48] Kalypso Nicolaidis and Rebecca Steffenson, "Managed Mutual Recognition in the Transatlantic Marketplace," p. 148.

[49] Gregory Shaffer, "Managing U.S.-EU Trade Relations Through Mutual Recognition and Safe Harbor Agreements: 'New' and 'Global' Approaches to Transatlantic Economic Governance?", 9 *Columbia Journal of European Law,* 29-77 (Fall 2002), p. 43.

[50] Stuart Eizenstad, op. cit. p. 26.

[51] Reinhardt Quick, "Regulatory Cooperation," p. 399.

[52] Reinhardt Quick, "Transatlantic Regulatory Cooperation on Chemicals—An Idealist's Dream?," German Marshall Fund Academic Policy Research Conference, May 8-9, 2008, Ford School, University of Michigan. Available at http://fordschool.umch.edu/nes/events_details/reg_coop_and_comp_08/.

[53] Testimony of Kathryn Hauser, U.S. Executive Director of the Transatlantic Business Dialogue, House Committee on Financial Services, "The U.S.-EU Economic Relationship: What Comes Next?," June 16, 2005, p. 9.

[54] Kalypso Nicolaidais and Rebecca Steffenson, p. 145.

[55] To co-chair the TEC, the Obama Administration appointed Michael Froman, Deputy National Security Advisor for International Economic Affairs, National Economic Council. The EU co-chair is the EU Trade Commissioner, Karel De Gucht.

[56] For more information on the TEC, see Section IV in the U.S.-EU Framework for Advancing Transatlantic Economic Integration, April 2007, available at http://www.whitehouse.gov/releases/2007/04/20070430-4.html.

[57] The Regulatory Cooperation Roadmap provides a framework of dialogues in 15 different sectors, including pharmaceuticals, telecommunications equipment, food safety, and auto safety.

[58] International Trade Reporter, "Transatlantic Council Meeting Advances Regulatory Cooperation, Innovative Strategies," 27 ITR 1963, December 23, 2010.

[59] See CRS Report RL34717, *Transatlantic Regulatory Cooperation: Background and Analysis*, pp. 7-9.

[60] For additional information, CRS Report RL34735, *Transatlantic Regulatory Cooperation: A Possible Role for Congress*, by Raymond J. Ahearn and Vincent Morelli.

[61] In December 2006, the Senate passed a resolution (S.Res. 632) calling for the completion of the Transatlantic Market by 2015. The resolution also called for a jointly funded, cooperatively led study of existing barriers to transatlantic trade and investment, including sector-by-sector estimates of the costs and benefits of removing such obstacles and a timetable for their removal.

[62] Congressman Henry Waxman, Hearing before the House Subcommittee on Oversight and Investigations of the Committee on Commerce, "Imported Drugs: U.S.-EU Mutual Recognition Agreement on Drug Prescriptions," 105th Congress, 2nd session, October 2, 1998, p. 4.

[63] Charan Devereaux, Robert Z. Lawrence, and Michael D. Watkins, "The U.S.-EU Mutual Recognition Agreements," p. 339.

[64] The TLD as currently structured does not include members of the Senate on the U.S. side. For more information on the role of the TLD, see pp. 10-16 of CRS Report RL34735, *Transatlantic Regulatory Cooperation: A Possible Role for Congress*, by Raymond J. Ahearn and Vincent Morelli.

In: U.S.- EU Regulatory Cooperation
Editor: William C. Ahrens

ISBN: 978-1-62100-745-6


*Chapter 2*

# TRANSATLANTIC REGULATORY COOPERATION: A POSSIBLE ROLE FOR CONGRESS[1]

***Raymond J. Ahearn and Vincent Morelli***

## SUMMARY

The United States and the European Union (EU) share a comprehensive, dynamic, and mutually beneficial economic relationship. Transatlantic markets are among the most open in the world and are deeply integrated. Although the global economic crisis has had a significant negative impact on the transatlantic economy, the great stake each side has had in the other's economy has afforded both sides the ability to withstand the worst of each other's current economic downturn. The key measure of the strength of the transatlantic relationship has been the ability of both sides to work with each other to weather the financial storm.

One issue that has worked against an even stronger economic relationship is the existence of regulatory barriers that limit a more integrated market from materializing. The United States and the EU have engaged in a number of attempts to reduce remaining non-tariff and regulatory barriers to trade. In the most recent effort, then President Bush and German Chancellor Merkel,

---

[1] [1] This is an edit, reformatted and augmented version of the Congressional Research Service Report for Congress RL34735.

serving as President of the EU, at the April 2007 U.S.-EU Summit agreed to establish the Transatlantic Economic Council (TEC). The TEC was directed to "advance the work of reducing or eliminating non-tariff barriers to transatlantic commerce and trade." The leaders also created an advisory group to "provide guidance and direction" to the TEC and invited the U.S. Congress, along with the European Parliament, to accept a new, more substantive role in transatlantic regulatory cooperation by becoming part of the advisory group. The Transatlantic Legislators' Dialogue (TLD), the formal exchange between Congress and the Parliament, was appointed to represent the legislatures in the TEC advisory group.

Since it began nearly two decades ago, transatlantic regulatory cooperation has been mostly limited to the executive branches and regulatory bodies on both sides of the Atlantic. However, the idea of legislators assuming a more proactive role in transatlantic economic and regulatory cooperation is not a new issue. At the 1995 launch of the New Transatlantic Agenda, the leaders of the United States and EU acknowledged that they "attached great importance to enhanced parliamentary links" and agreed to "consult with parliamentary leaders on both sides of the Atlantic regarding consultation mechanisms, including building on existing institutions, to discuss matters related to our transatlantic partnership." Advocates of the effort to achieve a more barrier-free transatlantic marketplace believe that ultimate success cannot be achieved without the strong commitment and active engagement of the U.S. Congress and the European Parliament.

Although the Transatlantic Legislators' Dialogue has been in existence formally since 1999, only recently have observers from both inside and outside of Congress gained familiarity with its structure, membership, and function. With respect to the role of Congress in the TEC process, several questions have been raised including the composition of the TLD, the role of the standing committees in both the Congress and the Parliament, the staff, and the role of the U.S. Senate. A number of options for enhancing the role of Congress and the structure of the TLD have been proposed.

This report provides background and analysis on the TEC process, the role of the Congress, and the TLD.

## INTRODUCTION

Since the end of the Cold War, the economies of the United States and Europe have experienced a period of accelerated integration interlinked by growing ties in trade, investment, and related employment.[1] Today, despite the recent global economic upheaval, the United States and the 27-member European Union (EU) continue to share a comprehensive, dynamic, and mutually beneficial economic partnership. Not only is the EU-U.S. commercial relationship, which advocates refer to as the transatlantic economy, the largest in the world, but for many practitioners in the transatlantic community it is also arguably the most important.[2]

Although hard hit by the current global economic downturn, the transatlantic economy continues to dominate the world economy by its sheer size and prosperity. The combined population of the United States and EU now approaches 800 million people who generate over half the world's production and are responsible for $4.4 trillion in commercial exchanges annually.[3] Transatlantic markets are among the most open in the world and are deeply integrated through investment flows, affiliate sales and related-party trade.[4] The transatlantic economy generates an estimated $4 trillion in commercial activity per year and accounts for close to 60% of global GDP and roughly 40% of world trade.[5] The United States and EU are each other's largest overall markets for a host of goods and services, ranging from agricultural products to high-tech goods and services. Large values of goods such as chemicals, transportation equipment, computers, and processed food as well as transportation and financial services are traded in record amounts.

More significant as the pillars of transatlantic commercial activity and the driving forces behind deepening transatlantic economic integration over the past decade have been foreign direct investment (FDI) and the interrelated activities of foreign affiliates.[6] In contrast to trade, mutual U.S. and European FDI results in "direct participation in each other's domestic economies."[7]

The fact that each side has a major ownership stake in the other's market may be the most distinctive aspect of the transatlantic economy. At the end of 2007, the total stock of two-way direct investment reached $2.7 trillion (composed of $1.4 trillion of U.S. direct investment in EU countries and $1.3 trillion of EU direct investments in the United States), making U.S. and European companies the largest investors in each other's market. Roughly 47% of all U.S. foreign direct investment is located in Europe, while EU member states supply 42% of global FDI in the United States. European affiliate income in the U.S. reached $82 billion in 2007 while U.S. affiliate income in Europe increased to $147 billion during that same period.[8] However, the global economic downturn has resulted in U.S. foreign affiliate income earned in Europe peaking in 2007 and actually declining by 2% by mid-2008. European affiliate earnings in the United States were reported to be flat in 2008.[9]

This massive amount of ownership of companies in each other's markets translates into billions of dollars of sales, profits, production, and expenditures on research and development. In addition, an estimated 6-7 million Americans are employed by European affiliates operating in the United States, and almost an equal number of EU citizens work for American companies in Europe.[10] In the current global economic crisis, these figures have declined somewhat but will still constitute significant transatlantic economic and financial activity.

The combined weight of these two economic superpowers means that how the United States and EU manage their relationship and the difficult issues involving domestic regulations, competition policy, and foreign investment often helps determine how the rest of the world deals with similar issues. As the figures might suggest, both the United States and EU have implemented policies that are receptive to expanding the commercial relationship. In theory, both sides have appeared to acknowledge that there is nothing to gain from protectionist investment policies. This theory is being tested in the current global financial environment as both sides of the Atlantic have flirted with some forms of protectionist policies (i.e., "buy America" provisions included in the U.S. stimulus legislation). Leaders in both Washington and Brussels have cautioned and urged restraint in implementing such policies seeking to ensure that cooperation which could help one another emerge from the current crisis is not impeded in any manner.

The success of economic integration achieved thus far, however, does not guarantee that the transatlantic economies will continue to deepen. The current global economic crisis has had a negative impact on the transatlantic economy. Regulatory irritants and barriers to greater commercial ties on both sides of the Atlantic remain to be adequately addressed. A key measure of the strength of the transatlantic relationship has been the ability of both sides to work with each other throughout the current financial storm in such a way that would permit further integration and would promote expanded regulatory cooperation, as both sides of the Atlantic begin to experience an economic recovery.

This report is intended to serve as a companion piece to CRS Report RL34717, *Transatlantic Regulatory Cooperation: Background and Analysis*, by Raymond J. Ahearn, which provides an introduction and primer on the issue of transatlantic regulatory cooperation.[11] The main focus of this report is on (1) the creation of the Transatlantic Economic Council; (2) the role of legislatures in the regulatory process; and (3) the Transatlantic Legislators' Dialogue and its new role as an advisor to transatlantic regulatory efforts.

## TRANSATLANTIC REGULATORY BARRIERS

Because many U.S. and European industries are already deeply integrated with each other and most tariffs are low, non-tariff and regulatory barriers are increasingly recognized as the most significant trade and investment impediments to the creation of a more integrated transatlantic market. A recent study carried out at the request of the European Parliament identifies non-Tariff Measures (NTM) in EU-US Trade and Investment that affect trade between the EU and the US, and estimates their economic impact.[12] NTMs are all about regulations, from product-specific technical standards to economy-wide regulations that may hamper trade. The purpose of the study was to estimate by how much regulatory differences increase the cost of doing business across the Atlantic, and to assess what impact they have on economic welfare in both economies. Estimates in the study were derived from a number of assumptions and were based in part on perceptions from industry; their translation into figures; an element of judgment on how to measure the impact of the reduction of individual NTMs and on whether and to what extent they can be reduced. In June 2005, a report issued by the Organization for Economic Cooperation and Development (OECD) estimated that certain structural reforms in both the United States and EU that included the reduction of competition-related regulations, tariff barriers, and restrictions on foreign direct investment could lead to permanent gains in GDP per capita on both sides of the Atlantic of up to 3 to 3.5 percent.[13]

However, some observers believe that while regulatory divergence does present an obstacle to trade, it does not automatically mean that the alignment of regulations in all sectors is possible or even desirable. In addition to domestic regulations, non-tariff barriers consist of elements such as safety norms, differences in health, environmental or engineering standards, rules of origin, or labeling requirements.[14] Such measures are due in part to different societal preferences and priorities, but also, to a significant degree, a lack of coordination or adequate information exchange between U.S. federal and state as well as EU and member state regulators and legislators on each side of the Atlantic all of whom are subject to different legal mandates or engaged in different oversight procedures.[15] One problem in addressing these different perspectives is the fact that the United States and Europe have very different regulatory processes and structures making attempts at regulatory convergence difficult.[16]

There have been a number of previous attempts to reduce existing non-tariff and regulatory barriers to trade. The aim of such efforts has been to reduce costs to businesses on both sides of the Atlantic, improve consumer welfare, and facilitate higher levels of economic growth. Attempts to seek meaningful regulatory cooperation began in 1995 when U.S. and European leaders launched the *New Transatlantic Agenda (NTA).* This initiative was designed to raise the U.S.-EU relationship to a new level of dialogue and decision-making in four areas including economic cooperation. Since then, the United States and the EU have launched several additional initiatives such as Mutual Recognition Agreements (1997), the Positive Economic Agenda (2002), the Transatlantic Economic Partnership (2004), and the Transatlantic Economic Agenda (2005) which included the formation of the High Level US-EU Regulatory Cooperation Forum. Each of these projects has contributed in some way to achieving limited progress towards reducing regulatory burdens. However, both European and U.S. companies heavily engaged in the transatlantic marketplace argue that the results have not proved materially significant. For instance, there seems to have been some improvements in areas such as competition policy and financial services, but progress in other areas such as chemicals has not been accomplished.[17]

## Creation of the Transatlantic Economic Council

In January 2007, German Chancellor Angela Merkel, upon assuming the rotating six-month presidency of the EU, proposed further liberalization of transatlantic trade and investment barriers by elevating the existing cooperation among U.S. and EU regulatory agencies. Building on the Merkel initiative, the April 2007 U.S.-EU Summit adopted a *Framework for Advancing Transatlantic Economic Integration.* The *framework* affirmed the importance of further deepening transatlantic economic integration, particularly through efforts to reduce or harmonize regulatory barriers to international trade and investment. A new institutional structure, a Transatlantic Economic Council (TEC), was established to advance the process of regulatory cooperation and barrier reduction by encouraging both U.S. and EU regulators to move forward on issues outlined in the *framework.*

The 2007 *Framework* presented the TEC with two priorities. The first was to build upon the established sectoral dialogues which had been taking place between U.S. and European Commission regulatory experts. These dialogues have included issues involving pharmaceuticals, automobile safety, cosmetics, consumer product safety, food safety, energy efficiency, and medical devices. The second priority was identified as the "Lighthouse Priority Projects." These included a review of policies on intellectual property rights and piracy, secure ports and trade, financial markets, innovation and technology, and investment.

The creation of the TEC was predicated on the premise that past efforts to achieve regulatory cooperation or convergence had been inadequate due to the technical nature of the work, the case-by-case, ad hoc approach, often assumed by regulatory agencies, and a lack of political leadership committed to having the regulators cooperate. The TEC is headed on both sides by ministerial-level appointees with cabinet rank.[18] Given that the two TEC leaders are cabinet-level appointees, the TEC was intended to have the high-level political support that previous efforts at economic integration may have lacked. Many observers believed the TEC, with its requirement to report annually to the U.S.-EU Summit, would receive that support. Such clout, it was argued, was needed to persuade domestic regulators to yield some of their authorities or to better cooperate with their counterparts across the Atlantic in harmonizing regulatory approaches.[19] After two years, however, there appears to be some concern among observers of the TEC that certain structural weaknesses in the TEC have limited its potential effectiveness. A recent report coauthored by the Atlantic Council and the Bertelsmann Foundation has recommended that the United States appoint the Vice President as the U.S. co-chair of the TEC and that the EU place responsibility for the TEC in the office of the EU President in an effort to upgrade the visibility and effectiveness of the TEC.[20]

The TEC, in theory, is designed to enable U.S. and European regulators to anticipate and discuss potential differences in thinking about new regulations before they become actual obstacles to transatlantic commerce. These efforts include a wide range of alternatives including dialogues and information exchanges among regulators, mutual recognition agreements, cost-benefit analysis, recommendations for voluntary principles, and proposals for binding agreements.

As part of its mandate, the TEC is to accelerate ongoing efforts to reduce or harmonize regulatory barriers. The TEC was directed to accomplish this mandate, in part, by including broader participation of stakeholders, including for the first time, legislators, in the discussions and meetings. In particular, the *framework* document instructed the TEC to establish an "advisory group" that draws upon the heads of the "existing transatlantic dialogues" to provide input and guidance on priorities for pursuing transatlantic economic integration. The existing transatlantic dialogues include the Transatlantic Legislators' Dialogue TLD, (the U.S. Congress-European Parliament exchange), the Transatlantic Business Dialogue (TABD), and the Transatlantic Consumers Dialogue (TACD). The TEC meets twice annually and reports to the annual U.S.-EU Summit on both achievements and areas where more progress is needed. To date, the advisory group has met with the TEC at each of the four TEC meetings held as of October 2009.

The first meeting of the TEC took place on November 9, 2007, in Washington, DC. A second meeting was held on May 13, 2008, in Brussels, and the third meeting took place on December 12, 2008, in Washington. For some observers, the results of these first meetings have been mixed. At the first meeting, the TEC agreed that in the field of financial accounting standards, both sides should pursue an agreement to accept the mutual recognition of each others accounting methods. At the second meeting, the TEC issued a joint statement affirming the commitment of both the United States and EU to promote open investment policies and to refrain from protectionist policies. The third meeting, the last of the Bush Administration, reviewed the operation of the TEC over its first 18 months and reaffirmed progress in areas such as investment and accounting standards, among others. The TEC also noted the importance of identifying issues suitable for TEC consideration and the need to avoid having the TEC agenda become too diffuse and unmanageable. The third TEC meeting convened in December 2008 as the global financial crisis began to have a significant impact on the transatlantic economy, highlighting for some the need for a stronger and more sustained transatlantic partnership.

The fourth meeting of the TEC was held on October 27, 2009, in Washington, DC. This meeting, the first of the Obama Administration and at the end of the EU Commission's five-year mandate, featured a significant deviation from previous meetings. At the October meeting, the TEC leadership met separately with each of the advisory groups, ostensibly to allow the U.S. side more time to explore how the TEC can move forward in the future in an effective way. However, with a new slate of EU Commissioners scheduled to be considered by the EU Parliament in late January 2010 there is some uncertainty about what the next Commissioner assigned to co-lead the TEC, Karel deGucht, would see as the EU's priorities and correspondingly how it might proceed in the future. Nevertheless, both sides committed the TEC to working more closely on energy related issues, services trade, financial regulatory compensation, and intellectual property rights. The TEC also agreed to set its next meeting for March 2010 and to develop plans to address issues such as innovation, labeling, and nanotechnology at that session.

The difficulty of harmonizing regulatory activities or resolving disputes embedded in regulatory differences, however, was underscored at all three of the earlier TEC meetings by the failure to resolve a long-standing dispute involving U.S. exports of poultry to the EU. The outcomes of the four meetings thus far, while not seen as resolving any of the regulatory issues before the TEC, have at least demonstrated that both sides remain committed to greater transatlantic economic integration and regulatory cooperation.

In January 2009, the Obama Administration came into office seeking to address both U.S. economic challenges as well as the global financial crisis. The Administration appeared to have acknowledged the importance of the transatlantic economic partnership and the potential role of the TEC when it relatively quickly designated Michael Froman, Deputy Director of the National Economic Council, as the Administration's point man for the TEC. In February, Mr. Froman met with the U.S. Director of the Transatlantic Business Dialogue, a major stakeholder in the TEC process, to discuss business issues and the future of the TEC.[21] President Obama also met with the EU leadership in Prague in early April 2009 and acknowledged the importance of energizing transatlantic ties and better coordinating policies to resolve the global economic downturn. Nevertheless, it took almost eight months to convene the first formal meeting of the TEC since the appointment of Mr. Froman.

For those advocates of the concept of a transatlantic marketplace free of artificial barriers and impediments to increased commercial and investment activity, the creation of the TEC was seen as a necessary measure. The goals and responsibilities established for the TEC as outlined by the U.S. and EU leadership seem designed to achieve that objective. According to some, the TEC promised to break new ground by enabling regular communication and exchange of information at a higher level on a variety of issues.[22] For others, the TEC may be at a crossroads when the central role as a forum for discussing strategic issues and a facilitator of renewed economic growth between the U.S. and Europe, has to make a break from single-issue gridlock, such as the poultry dispute, that has bogged down the TEC.[23]

One question that is raised is why regulatory cooperation should be done just in the context of transatlantic relations. Some advocates point out that many of these regulatory issues, such as regulating financial services industries, are global in nature and apply to regions such as Asia and Latin America, as well as Europe. For many, this is a legitimate question and is answered by some who point out that as highly developed economic systems, both the United States and the EU, could set the global standards for future regulation in broad economic categories.

The dilemma for the TEC, then, may continue to be the uncertainty over its role. Is the TEC to be a dispute settlement body putting out fires in transatlantic trade or is it primarily designed to promote regulatory convergence? This question has been given new relevance with the formation of the new EU Commission. Under the new Commission, responsibility for the TEC has been shifted from the Director General(DG) for Enterprise and Industry to DG for Trade. The TEC also seems limited in its structure to deal with national interests or to overcome domestic political opposition to items on its agenda which is why some have suggested that the U.S. appoint a "sherpa" from the National Security Council and include the OMB in coordinating U.S. positions.[24] Whether the TEC will prove a more successful entity for actually accomplishing a reduction in remaining transatlantic regulatory and non-tariff barriers to trade remains uncertain.[25]

## The Role of the Legislatures

Since it began nearly two decades ago, transatlantic regulatory cooperation has been mostly limited to the executive branches and regulatory bodies on both sides of the Atlantic except when the U.S. Congress has adopted legislation with significant regulatory impact such as was the case with passage of the Sarbanes-Oxley reform bill. However, the idea of legislators assuming a more proactive role in transatlantic economic and regulatory cooperation is not a new issue. At the 1995 launch of the New Transatlantic Agenda, the leaders of the United States and EU acknowledged that they "attached great importance to enhanced parliamentary links" and agreed to "consult with parliamentary leaders on both sides of the Atlantic regarding consultation mechanisms, including building on existing institutions, to discuss matters related to our transatlantic partnership."[26] For those interested in the transatlantic economic relationship, this broad mandate to include the legislators has resulted in an increased interest in the role the U.S. Congress and the European Parliament can or should play in regulatory cooperation and convergence. In fact, the implementation of the EU's new Lisbon treaty will give the European Parliament more decision-making authority over trade related issues and possibly an enlarged role in regulatory decision making or oversight.

Many Representatives of Congress and the European Parliament have long argued for greater legislative participation in broader U.S.-EU relations including such matters and participation in the annual U.S.–EU Summit process. Numerous pieces of legislation have been introduced and even passed in both Congress and the Parliament over the past seven years calling for enhanced dialogue and coordination between the Congress and the European Parliament in matters related to the transatlantic economic relationship. In 2004 and 2005, the European Parliament passed resolutions supporting the completion of the transatlantic market by 2015. In 2006 the U.S. Senate passed a similar resolution in S.Res. 632.

## Rationale for Including the Legislatures

Despite the NTA declaration regarding participation of legislators, and past legislative initiatives approved by Congress and the Parliament, incorporating the legislatures into the regulatory process has been met with questions and mixed views. Advocates of the effort to achieve a more barrier-free transatlantic marketplace believe that ultimate success cannot be achieved without the strong commitment and active engagement of the U.S. Congress and the European Parliament. Some of these advocates have decried the low level of engagement by Congress and the Parliament thus far in the overall economic integration and regulatory cooperation process and believe congressional committees need to be more active in the oversight process. These groups believe that, through more active oversight, Congress can articulate its support for, or concerns about, a particular regulatory direction before the regulators proceed too far down the negotiation path. They believe more enhanced oversight could serve to help Congress and the Parliament develop as stronger partners by understanding at an earlier stage, the rationale for traveling or not traveling down a certain regulatory path.

These advocates also believe Congress, through its authorization and appropriation roles, can prod the regulators to move the cooperative efforts forward and can provide the funds necessary to carry out that mandate. Some within this group have even suggested going further and inviting legislators to actively participate in high-level regulatory dialogues in addition to their role in the TEC advisory group.[27] Those in this general camp point to the "open skies" agreement laboriously negotiated between the United States and EU, which was intended to make airline travel to and from and within both Europe and the United States more competitive. One key provision, which would have allowed 49% foreign ownership of U.S. airlines, was drastically scaled back at the eleventh hour by congressional action. Supporters of this agreement felt this outcome might have been avoided had Congress been included in the process at an earlier stage. Now that the EU has suggested that negotiations begin on a follow-on aviation agreement in 2010, some believe this could be a good test for enhanced participation of the Congress and the Parliament.

On the other hand, there are many in the business and regulatory communities who are concerned about the autonomy of the U.S. regulatory process even though that process is sometimes influenced by legislative direction and worry that the involvement of legislators in the TEC process could undermine the sovereignty of both the U.S. and European regulatory processes. These groups accept the congressional and Parliament responsibility to conduct oversight. However, some in this group seem reluctant to encourage more active engagement of legislators in the regulatory reform process beyond oversight hearings. This group does not believe Congress or the Parliament is at the point politically where they are willing to discuss proposed regulatory changes in the context of the impact on the transatlantic relationship. These skeptics point to the recent U.S. economic stimulus legislation which subjected some funds to "Buy America" restrictions, despite the understanding that U.S. economic recovery can only be successful if the global economy is also improving and willing to buy U.S. products. These skeptics also point to the recent expressions of concern over free trade and globalization, and the recent negative reaction to European participation in the Air Force air refueling acquisition program as indications that further transatlantic economic integration may not yet be a concept that is fully accepted by a majority of the Congress. This group also raises concerns of what happens when the legislatures decide to take, what for some would be regulatory matters, into their own hands without close consultation with transatlantic regulatory bodies or the outside stakeholders that may be impacted. This group has referred to the Sarbanes-Oxley legislation passed by Congress or the Registration, Evaluation, and Authorization of Chemicals (REACH) directive adopted by the European Parliament, as examples of well intentioned initiatives that have ultimately caused some regulatory problems that affected the transatlantic relationship. Many doubt, however, that the TEC process could have prevented such legislative actions no matter how engaged the regulators were with the legislatures at the time these issues arose.

Finally, some believe that involving the legislators as advisors alongside the business and consumer communities is not an appropriate role for legislators who may be called upon to make changes to legislation, such as the

100% cargo screening requirement, or to introduce new legislation in order to accomplish the TEC agenda.[28]

## Concerns with the Legislatures

Not every regulatory proposal on the U.S.-EU agenda would need legislative action by Congress. But the ability of Congress or the Parliament to disapprove of, reverse through legislation, or prohibit the expenditure of funds to implement a regulatory change is a power that has been recognized and which must be considered.

One problem that has arisen since 1995 regarding the dialogue with the legislators, at least in the United States, has been that successive Administrations have had difficulty deciding who it is to consult with, how to do it, and when. No single congressional committee exercises jurisdiction over the broad array of issues on the regulatory agenda. And, the committees that have the primary authority to oversee the transatlantic political relationship, the House Foreign Affairs Committee under House Rule X and the Senate Foreign Relations Committee under Senate Rule XXV have no authority on the specific regulatory issues under consideration.

Another concern that is raised is the question of whether the legislators, themselves, are prepared to take on a more substantive partnership in the transatlantic regulatory process. Given the nature of regulatory cooperation, the multiple layers of agencies involved, the sometimes slow pace of reform, and normal legislative demands, some observers feel the Congress may not be adequately prepared to apply a transatlantic dimension to this process. To address these concerns, the decision taken in the House in 2000 to create a Subcommittee in the then International Relations Committee solely dedicated to Europe, along with the formation of a Members Caucus on the EU in 2005, have provided important new venues for a more focused discussion of transatlantic relations that now must be energized. Beginning with the launch of the New Transatlantic Agenda, organizations such as the Transatlantic Policy Network, the German Marshall Fund and other think-tanks and public policy groups, have become more involved in developing the transatlantic knowledge base of the Congress. Publications, such as the annual transatlantic economic report, issued by the Center for Transatlantic Relations, have served to bring the economic message to the forefront. Ongoing efforts by groups such as the Transatlantic Business Dialogue, the U.S. Chamber of Commerce and the European-American Business Council have injected more specificity to the debate. Two recent reports, the previously referenced Atlantic Council/Bertlesman report on the TEC and a report co-authored by several U.S. and European "think-tanks" entitled, "Shoulder to Shoulder: Forging a Strategic U.S.-EU Partnership"[29] has helped to define the parameters that a regulatory cooperation dialogue should take in 2010.

The attempt by these outside organizations to increase the level of awareness and interest among at least a portion of the Congress, including within congressional committees that have jurisdiction over the issues involved, seems to have begun to have an impact on both regulatory cooperation and transatlantic relations. Most observers understand that the transatlantic impact of legislation is rarely a central consideration during the legislative process. Nor do many believe Congress would submit its own legislative initiatives to any form of a transatlantic impact statement or cede its authority to react to a national crisis, such as a terrorist attack, banking or corporate failure, without first consulting the EU. Some in Congress are not sure what their role in the transatlantic regulatory process should be. Even those Members of Congress initially contacted and asked to participate in the TEC advisory group had expressed uncertainty over their role and continue to seek more clarity on exactly what they are expected to provide to the TEC.[30]

Nevertheless, some observers believe the efforts to elevate congressional awareness of the expanding U.S.-EU partnership, the magnitude of the transatlantic economic relationship, and the increasing dialogue involving transatlantic economic integration and regulatory cooperation over the past several years has begun to pay off through a more notable desire by some in Congress to become more engaged in that process.

The TEC was created by those who supported the importance of a structured, institutionalized dialogue between the transatlantic business and consumer communities, the European Parliament, and the U.S. Congress. Supporters anticipate that under this structure, legislators can become more aware of the potential impact on transatlantic trade and investment stemming from their legislative work and may be more sensitive to initiatives that might strengthen or undermine further transatlantic economic integration efforts.[31] Skeptics, however, maintain that the danger here is that the TEC process, with legislative participation, could serve to slow or even undermine regulatory integration efforts.

# THE TRANSATLANTIC LEGISLATORS' DIALOGUE

## History

According to the Transatlantic Legislators' Dialogue (TLD) website[32] (found only on the European Parliament's website), formal exchanges between the U.S. House of Representatives and the European Parliament can be traced back to 1972, when the first group of Members of the House traveled to Brussels for the express purpose of meeting and exchanging views with the Parliament. Apparently at the time, the Congress viewed the European Communities as mostly a commercial and trade arrangement with the authority to negotiate trade agreements and thus, the first visits to Brussels appear to have been arranged by Members of the House Committee on Ways and Means. These Members were most interested in issues such as agriculture subsidies, steel tariffs, and anti-dumping initiatives. This parliamentary exchange, which only involved the House, became known as the US-EU Community Inter-parliamentary Group. Since 1972, with few exceptions, the parliamentary exchange has met twice annually, once in the United States and once in Europe.

Given the broad transatlantic nature of the exchange, and the changes gradually taking place within the EU itself, the annual meetings gradually focused more on a foreign policy agenda dedicated to the issues involving the cold war and the evolving nature of the European Union. By 1989, the responsibility for arranging the US-EU meetings in the U.S. and the congressional delegations to Europe rested in the House Foreign Affairs Committee under the leadership of former representatives Benjamin Gilman and Tom Lantos. In response to the launch of the New Transatlantic Agenda in 1995, the delegations of the U.S. House and the European Parliament, at their 50th meeting in January 1999 agreed to change the group's name to the Transatlantic Legislators' Dialogue. In announcing the formation of the TLD, the two delegations stated that the Dialogue "will constitute the formal response of the European Parliament and the U.S. Congress to the commitment in the New Transatlantic Agenda to enhance parliamentary ties between the European Union and the United States."[33] In response to the decision to change the group's name to the Transatlantic Legislators' Dialogue, the U.S. House in November 1999, during consideration of the

Consolidated Appropriations Act for Fiscal Year 2000 (H.R. 3194/P.L. 106-113), amended Section 109(c) of the Department of State Authorization Act for Fiscal Years 1984/1985 (22U.S.C. 276) to officially change the name of the group. Since then the TLD's agenda for each meeting has included a broader discussion of economic and trade issues, and more recently to its role as a potential influence in the transatlantic regulatory process.

Although formal engagement between the U.S. House and the European Parliament has occurred regularly for some 36 years, some observers believe the TLD remains little known or understood both within and outside the House, although this may be changing. This has been disappointing to some because over the past years many delegations have traveled to Europe and several senior Members of the House have participated in exchange activities or knew of the exchange sessions. For instance, in 1987, then-Speaker Jim Wright attended the exchange meetings in Madrid. Between 1994 and 2000, the Chairman of the House International Relations Committee also served as the U.S. Chairman of the TLD. In 2007, the visiting EU TLD delegation was received by House Speaker Pelosi and Senate Majority Leader Reid.[34]

The lack of knowledge of the TLD seemed to contribute to the surprise of many in the transatlantic community when the TEC leadership invited the TLD to be a key member of its Advisory Group. In fact, there has been little evidence that anyone at the White House at the time of the 2007 U.S.-EU Summit thought to inform the House leadership that the Administration was about to unilaterally assign a new role to the legislative branch. Nor did it appear prior to the announcement in the summer of 2007 that anyone had informed the USTLD Chair that the group was to be handed a new, rather far-reaching responsibility—that of formally representing the views of Congress in the transatlantic economic integration and regulatory cooperation process.[35]

According to some, the initial lack of familiarity with the TLD, its membership, its function, and its understanding of the TEC process, might have been due to the fact that unlike several other parliamentary exchanges that operate in the Congress, such as the NATO Parliamentary Assembly or the British-American Parliamentary Group, the TLD has never been statutorily authorized. Apparently, this circumstance had caused some concern within the transatlantic community with respect to the TLD's ability to carry out its new role as advisor to the TEC. Although the TLD continues to lack statutory standing, it appears more and more attention is being paid to the TLD, or at least the Congress, by those committed to the TEC process. The October unveiling of the previously mentioned Atlantic Council/Bertelsmann report on the TEC at a meeting of Members and staff in the U.S. House served as a recognition of the importance of the Congress in this process.

More recently, however, the TLD has received renewed attention. At a December 15, 2009, hearing of the House Europe Subcommittee, the importance of Congressional-EU Parliament exchanges in general and the TLD in particular were given considerably more public attention than in previous years, including an endorsement by the Subcommittee Chairman, who has been a long-time supporter of increased contact between the Congress and the EU Parliament.

## The TLD Structure

One question which has risen in the past has been the issue of what Members actually belong to the TLD. In the European Parliament there is a formal group of 32 members that constitute the Delegation for Relations with the United States. Participants to the TLD meetings are drawn from this delegation. In the U.S. Congress, other than the appointment of the Chair and Vice-Chair by the Chairman and Ranking Member of the House Foreign Affairs Committee, there is no formal nomination of any other USTLD member. While many Members have participated in past meetings, participation in the USTLD often seemed to be on an ad hoc basis, involving little continuity of participants and, in some instances, largely dependent on the ability of the Chairman to convince Members to attend the annual meetings.[36]

Although participation in TLD sessions appears lately to have reached a significant level of continuity, there is still a concern among some observers that the TLD continues to have difficulty attracting and maintaining a broad group of Members willing to participate on a permanent basis. This is an important issue for many because frank and open exchanges of views often come more easily through long-term relationships that rely on personal interactions developed between legislators over time and through familiarity. Often it seems that regular communication only takes place between the U.S. and EU Chairs or their staff. Some EU participants have observed that if they had a particular issue that was of interest to them they might not know any other member of the U.S. delegation that they could contact for discussion. There have also been attempts to promote on-going dialogues between U.S. and EU TLD members through the use of video conferences so that TLD members can keep in touch between regular meetings. For the transatlantic business and consumer community this also presents a problem in that there is no permanently established group of TLD members with whom these outside interest groups can meet to discuss issues on the regulatory agenda on a regular basis.[37]

There have been several ideas put forward to help restructure the TLD. For instance in the previously mentioned report, "Shoulder to Shoulder", the authors suggested that the TLD include members from both the House and Senate and that the House members be appointed by the Speaker. Another suggestion advocated by others involves creating a political committee and an economic committee within the TLD. Members from both the U.S. and European delegations would be assigned as Chairs and Vice-Chairs of each. Rapporteurs might also be assigned to report on specific issues. This structure would at least offer Members/MEPs of the TLD the opportunity to focus some of their attention on issues for which they may have a particular interest or expertise. The committee Chairs would report to the entire body at some point during the TLD meetings on the issues discussed in the committees. Assigning Members/MEPs as Chairs, Vice-Chairs, and rapporteurs would also convey a sense of responsibility within the TLD and could guarantee a more consistent group of attendees.

A second question that has been raised involves the capacity of the TLD, as currently structured, to dedicate more time and effort to addressing those economic and regulatory issues that will appear on the TEC agenda and how the TLD will interface with standing committees of jurisdiction. While the TLD, at its past annual meetings, has engaged in a broad discussion of issues, foreign policy matters often seemed to dominate the agenda. However, the Chairs of the TLD did include the more specific TEC process as a regular agenda item beginning with the April 2009 meeting held in Prague. The elections for the European Parliament held in June 2009 resulted in a new EU leadership that met in December 2009 in New York City. It appears that the perspective from the EU parliamentarians will remain consistent with respect to ideas for how the TLD should operate in the future.

Some observers fear, however, that as the regulatory dialogue proceeds on issues such as the mutual recognition of accounting standards, supply chain security, copyright and patent protection, preferred traveler programs, cosmetics testing and medical device certification, an unstructured TLD may find itself further down the learning curve than its transatlantic business and consumer partners in the TEC and may find that it needs to spend a great deal of time catching up on the issues. This could present a problem for some members of the TLD who may be reluctant to become more specialized in economic and regulatory matters at the expense of other broader transatlantic policy issues. These members would not want the TLD to become strictly TEC oriented.

## Role of the Committees[38]

With respect to the committees of jurisdiction, until the beginning of the 111th Congress the current USTLD Chair and Vice Chair sat on the Trade Subcommittees of the House Committee on Ways and Means and the Committee on Energy and Commerce, respectively, positions from which they both could speak on trade and regulatory issues. Neither, however, sat on the Foreign Affairs Committee which has jurisdiction over the TLD. This situation changed with the new Congress when the U.S. Chair was appointed to the Committee on Foreign Affairs and its Europe Subcommittee but lost her seat on the trade subcommittee. From the position of this new assignment, the U.S. Chair is able to address the broader issue of transatlantic relations and the specific issues of regulatory cooperation with the EU. Despite the greater connection between the USTLD Chair and the Foreign Affairs Committee, it still remains unclear whether other committees, such as the House Committee on Financial Services, the Committee on the Judiciary, or the Committee on Homeland Security that have jurisdiction over issues such as financial services, technology innovation, intellectual property and homeland security will defer to the TLD to provide advice and guidance to the TEC on behalf of those committees or how an information sharing process between the TLD and the committees would be accomplished. This issue was somewhat addressed at the recent meeting between the TLD leadership and the TEC leadership when a member of the Financial Services Committee, which is deeply engaged in new financial services regulation, participated in the discussions. It is important that Committees that have jurisdiction over issues potentially on the TEC agenda be included in these sessions because when the TEC meets and issues its recommendations on how the U.S. and EU might deal with issues such as the mutual recognition of accounting standards, poultry, consumer product safety or port security functions, they will likely do so with what they believe will have been the best guidance, not from two or three individual Members of Congress or EU Parliament who happen to be the TLD Chairs and Vice-Chairs, but from the House of Representatives and the Parliament as a whole. The challenge, then, for the TLD continues to be how to develop a relationship with the appropriate House and Senate standing committees, and the House and Senate Leadership for that matter, that would provide for a useful exchange of views on what the Committees are thinking on the issues under consideration by the TEC and how the TLD can present those views formally to the U.S. executive branch and European Commission with some degree of authority without at the same time diminishing the traditional and rightful authority of the Committees.

## Staffing the TLD

A third question for those actively engaged in the transatlantic regulatory process seems to involve the issue of who the business and consumer communities should deal with at the congressional staff level on an everyday basis for issues related to the TEC process. On the U.S. side, there are two principal staff assigned to the TLD with one designated the "U.S. secretariat." These staff are part of the House Foreign Affairs Committee structure and have their own portfolio of responsibilities beyond the TLD. Observers note that while the Foreign Affairs Committee staff are highly professional for what they do for the committee and knowledgeable of transatlantic relations, none of the top issues listed in the U.S.-EU "framework" or those likely to be addressed by the TEC over the next few years, are issues that fall under Rule X of the Foreign Affairs Committee. For some observers, it may be a real stretch to expect that Foreign Affairs staff who are responsible for following issues and events in places like Georgia, Kosovo, Ukraine, and elsewhere throughout Europe can somehow also find the time to become proficient on automobile crash testing, container scanning, toy safety or hedge fund transparency. Realistically, it would also seem that neither the Foreign Affairs Committee nor the TLD Co-Chairs could hire a whole cadre of staff with the kind of expertise needed to be responsive to the TEC process.

For the transatlantic business and consumer community it is unclear how they are to work with the staff of the committees of jurisdiction on the specific technicalities of a TEC agenda while at the same time working with the Foreign Affairs Committee staff assigned to the TLD. The Atlantic Council-Bertelsmann "Blueprint" suggests that in order to optimize legislative participation in the TEC, some type of Committee designated "coordinators" must work with the TLD secretariats as a way to allow the staff of the TLD to tap into the expertise of the professional staff of the committees that exercise jurisdiction over these issues. This may be difficult currently as it appears many committee staff outside of the Foreign Affairs committee are unfamiliar with the TLD, the TEC, or the new congressional responsibility as an advisor to the transatlantic regulatory process and may be less inclined to share the work they are doing for their committees with the staff of the TLD.[39] This recommendation is also problematic because it implies that the staff of the Foreign Affairs Committee covering the TLD will have the time to meet with multiple "coordinators" to discuss issues related to those committees of jurisdiction.

### Role of the Senate

Finally, some observers have raised the question of what role the Senate will play in this process. The fact that the Senate has a co-equal role in regulatory oversight, but is not included as part of the TLD, seems to have been missed by the decision makers who agreed to include the TLD in the TEC Advisory Group. As of October 2009, the TEC has met for four sessions with the Advisory Group yet there does not seem to be a formal mechanism within the TLD to include the Senate in its activities nor within the TEC Advisory Group to solicit Senate opinion. For instance, while the TEC leadership met with the TLD leadership in the House on October 27, 2009, for one hour as part of the TEC advisory process, it appears that neither TEC co-chairs met with any Member of the Senate to discuss their work. Thus, while the TLD over time could develop some level of authority to represent the views of the House on issues addressed in the Advisory Group's meetings with the TEC, the TLD, as currently structured, could not claim to speak on behalf of the Senate. This oversight will have to be addressed if the TEC intends to receive the advice of the whole Congress. In fact, at a December hearing of the Europe Subcommittee in the Senate, the issue of the TLD and the role of the Senate in the TEC process was addressed by the witnesses and, according to Committee staff, will apparently be further investigated.

## Structural Options

Most observers of the TEC process thus far maintain that the Transatlantic Business Dialogue (TABD) and the Transatlantic Consumer Dialogue (TACD) can and will support the TEC process even as both organizations have been critical of certain aspects of transatlantic regulatory cooperation. There is, however, uncertainty about the role of Congress and its representative, the

TLD. The TLD is an inter-parliamentary entity, and as such, does not have, at this point, a mandate to formally represent Congress as a whole or even the House separately. Until the TLD and Congress itself, have a better understanding of what is expected of it and how it will carry out its mandate as an advisor to the TEC, doubts will remain. Some engaged in the transatlantic regulatory process have suggested that the TLD as a whole, and the USTLD specifically, be restructured in order to make it a more effective partner in the TEC advisory role. At the very least, this group believes the TLD should be formally authorized and given a status slightly different than the other parliamentary groups in the Congress.[40] There are several options which the TLD, itself, could explore in an attempt to make it more responsive.

One option that would allow the TLD to continue its broad mandate to address all transatlantic issues and at the same time fulfill its role as a TEC advisor, may be for the U.S. and EU TLD co-chairs to announce the creation of their own TLD/ TEC Working Group or Groups. The co-chairs could appoint one U.S. and one EU member who have regularly attended the TLD meetings to co-chair the group. The co-chairs would recruit other regular TLD participants or members of the appropriate committees of jurisdiction for the working group(s). In the case of the USTLD, recruitment could also come from groups such as the EU Caucus. Other than the co-chairs, the members of this group would not have to agree to join the TLD on a regular basis but would work closely with other standing committee members, the TEC, and the two other advisory partners, the TABD and the TACD. The working group(s) would brief the TLD co-chairs prior to any formal meeting of the TEC. The U.S. working group co-chair(s) could also attempt to reach out to colleagues in the Senate to help provide Senate input into this process. The downside of this option may be the fact that recommendations to the TEC would still come from an inter-parliamentary group that, while reflective of the views of their wider legislative bodies, would still not have a mandate to speak on behalf of those bodies.

A second option might involve the TLD reaching out to the members of groups with similar interests, such as the Transatlantic Policy Network (TPN) which includes members of both the House and Senate. The TPN, which is a mix of legislators and private sector representatives, already has a Task Force on the Bi-lateral Economic Partnership. The TLD could invite that TPN Task Force to serve as an informal advisor to the TLD. The co-chairs of the TPN Task Force are Members of Congress and the European Parliament and several of the TPN members have participated in past TLD meetings. Much of the work of the Bi-lateral Economic Task Force mirrors the work of the TEC with respect to regulatory reform. The TPN Task Force would continue with its own independent work which could be shared with the TEC, but periodically, the co-chairs and/or their staff could meet with the TLD co-chairs and/or their staff to share ideas, information and recommendations. A briefing for the TLD co-chairs by the TPN Task Force could be arranged in advance of each TEC meeting. The TPN Task Force could also be invited to make a formal presentation to the regular TLD meetings. Downsides of this option would again be the issue of a parliamentary group speaking for Congress, whether the TPN would be willing to share its work with the TLD, and the fact that the TPN Task Force may not include key Committee Chairmen who would be omitted from the process.

A third option could involve the Chair and Vice-Chair of the USTLD requesting that the House and Senate Leadership appoint a special bi-partisan, bi-cameral, "Regulatory Cooperation Advisory Group" to the TLD. This group would consist of the TLD leadership plus representatives of the appropriate House and Senate standing committees, including committee or subcommittee chairmen with jurisdiction over the issues identified as being of interest to the TEC. This advisory group and their committee staff would follow the work of the TEC through the agencies these committees oversee. Periodic meetings between the TEC staff and committee staff could take place to update the TEC process. Once an agenda is clarified for an upcoming TEC meeting, the TLD Chair and Vice-Chair could convene only those advisory group members whose issues were identified on the TEC agenda. Such a Leadership appointed advisory group would elevate the TEC process and the TLD role to a higher level to one that would now include the House and Senate Leadership as a stakeholder in the process. The downsides to this option could include the potential conflict between the legislatures and the regulators over agenda setting, the potential for partisan conflict due to the make up of the advisory group to the TLD, and disagreements over jurisdiction among the committees.

Whether any of these options, or others are pursued, some observers of the TEC process who support Congressional participation in the Advisory Group believe the TEC would receive a real boost if the Obama Administration sent a clear signal to the Congressional leadership that the role of the Congress in the transatlantic regulatory cooperation process was important and that a stronger representation from the Congress through an enhanced TLD participation in the TEC Advisory Group would be welcome. The fact that the October 2009 meeting of the TEC did include a separate meeting, on the Hill, between the TEC leadership and the TLD leadership may have been an opening move for such an Administration strategy.

# CONCLUSION

As the TEC process attempts to move regulatory cooperation toward the ultimate goal of a well-functioning, unencumbered transatlantic marketplace, the role the Congress will or should actually play has raised several questions among those participating in that process. These issues have led many observers to believe that the TLD, although never intended to be anything more than a mechanism for exchanging views among parliamentarians, currently welds little influence or authority as a transatlantic policy resource and in not a representative of Congress' views on economic integration. Nevertheless, the decision to include an advisory group with representation from the transatlantic legislative communities, through the Transatlantic Legislators' Dialogue, has been viewed by some as a real opportunity for the Congress and Parliament to assume a more direct role as a stakeholder in the long-term development and completion of the transatlantic marketplace. Despite some short-comings in the current structure of the USTLD, all indications are that the current Chair and Vice Chair, along with their counterpart EU Chair, are fully committed to making the TLD a more active partner in the TEC process.[41]

If the identified concerns with the TLD, along with its responsibilities as a member of the TEC Advisory Group are more fully addressed, the TLD might become an organization capable of taking on a more substantive role in regulatory cooperation. For many observers, this could lead the TLD to become, over time, a more important stakeholder in regulatory cooperation and a voice for transatlantic relations in the Congress. In the near term, however, these observers believe the TLD's role as a force for the promotion of greater transatlantic economic integration and regulatory cooperation, on behalf of the U.S. Congress, will remain its greatest challenge.

## End Notes

[1] James Elles, *"The Transatlantic Market: A Reality by 2015?,"* Transatlantic Policy Network, 2006.

[2] For Background on U.S. -EU commercial ties see CRS Report RL30608, *EU-U.S. Economic Ties: Framework, Scope, and Magnitude*, by William H. Cooper; and CRS Report RL34381, *European Union-U.S. Trade and Investment Relations: Key Issues*, coordinated by Raymond J. Ahearn.

[3] Cited in a speech by Catherine Ashton at the U.S. Chamber of Commerce, Washington, DC., October 26, 2009.

[4] Daniel S. Hamilton, *"Creating the Transatlantic Marketplace,"* Commentary Section, American Institute for Contemporary German Studies, 2008.

[5] Daniel Hamilton and Joseph Quinlan, *"The Transatlantic Economy 2008,"* American Chamber of Commerce-EU and the Center for Transatlantic Relations, 2008.

[6] James Elles, op. cit.

[7] The Atlantic Council of the United States, "The Transatlantic Economy in 2020: A Partnership for the Future?" Policy Paper, 2004, p.2.

[8] *Completing the Transatlantic Market,* 2nd Annual Report, Transatlantic Policy Network, May 2008.

[9] Center for Transatlantic Relations, Johns Hopkins University, *The Transatlantic Economy 2009, Executive Summary,* by Daniel S. Hamilton and Joseph P. Quinlan. Available at http://transatlantic.sais-jhu.edu

[10] Center for Transatlantic Relations, Johns Hopkins University, *The Transatlantic Economy2008, Executive Summary,* by Daniel S. Hamilton and Joseph P. Quinlan.

[11] See CRS Report RL34717, *Transatlantic Regulatory Cooperation: Background and Analysis*, by Raymond J. Ahearn.

[12] "Non-Tariff Measures in EU-US Trade and Investment: An Economic Analysis", Ecorys Nederland, BV, December 18, 2009. This study was prepared for the European Commission's Director General for Trade.

[13] OEDC, "The Benefits of Liberalizing Product Markets and Reducing Barriers to International Trade and Investment: The Case of the United States and the European Union," *Economics Department Working Paper 432,* Paris, May/June 2005.

[14] See CRS Report RL34717, *Transatlantic Regulatory Cooperation: Background and Analysis*, by Raymond J. Ahearn, pp. 2-4.

[15] Daniel S. Hamilton, "*Creating the Transatlantic Marketplace,"* Commentary Section, American Institute for Contemporary German Studies, 2008

[16] CRS Report RL34717, *Transatlantic Regulatory Cooperation: Background and Analysis*, by Raymond J. Ahearn, op. cit., pp.8-10.

[17] CRS Report RL34717, *Transatlantic Regulatory Cooperation: Background and Analysis*, by Raymond J. Ahearn, op. cit., pp.14-19.

[18] To chair the TEC, the U.S. side initially named Alan Hubbard, Assistant to the President for Economic Policy and Director of the National Economic Council, and the EU appointed Gunter Verheugen, Vice President of the European Commission and Commissioner for Enterprise and Industry. David Price, Assistant to the President for International Economic Affairs succeeded Hubbard. The Obama Administration appointed Michael Froman, Deputy National Security Advisor for International Economic Affairs, National Economic Council as U.S. TEC chair.

[19] For more information on the TEC, see Section IV in the U.S.-EU Framework for Advancing Transatlantic Economic Integration, April 2007, available at http://www.whitehouse.gov/news/releases/2007/04/20070430-4.html, and CRS Report RL34717, *Transatlantic Regulatory Cooperation: Background and Analysis*, by Raymond J. Ahearn, op. cit., p.20

[20] *Resetting The Trans-Atlantic Economic Council, A BluePrint,"* A Report By the Atlantic Council and Bertelsmann Foundation, October 2009.

[21] Conversation with the Executive Director of the Transatlantic Business Dialogue.

[22] Daniel S. Hamilton, op. cit., p.4.

[23] *Resetting the Trans-Atlantic Economic Council,* p.1.

[24] Ibid., p. 9.

[25] CRS Report RL34717, *Transatlantic Regulatory Cooperation: Background and Analysis*, by Raymond J. Ahearn, op. cit., pp.20-22.

[26] Declaration of the New Transatlantic Agenda at the U.S. -EU Summit, December 13, 1995.

[27] See the American Chamber of Commerce to the EU(AMCHAMEU) position paper, "Advancing Transatlantic Economic Integration," October 2007.

[28] Comments presented by the U.S. Chamber of Commerce and Business Europe to the TEC, October 1, 2008.
[29] Shoulder to Shoulder: Forging a Strategic U.S.-EU Partnership", Atlantic Council of the United States, the Center for Transatlantic Relations, et al, December 2009.
[30] CRS interviews with congressional staff.
[31] Transatlantic Economic Council, *Report to the EU-U.S. Summit*, April 2008.
[32] Information on the TLD can be found at http://www.europarl.europa.eu/intcoop/tld/default_en.htm.
[33] Joint statement of the delegations of the U.S. Congress and the European Parliament, January 16, 1999.
[34] See the TLD website for additional information.
[35] CRS interviews with congressional staff.
[36] CRS interviews with congressional staff.
[37] CRS interviews with representatives of the business community.
[38] For a listing of congressional committees involved see CRS Report RL34717, *Transatlantic Regulatory Cooperation: Background and Analysis*, by Raymond J. Ahearn, pp. 26-27.
[39] CRS staff discussions and interviews with Congressional staff.
[40] Some in the business community have discussed the option of promoting legislation that would formalize the TLD's role in the TEC process.
[41] CRS interviews with congressional staff.

In: U.S.- EU Regulatory Cooperation
Editor: William C. Ahrens
ISBN: 978-1-62100-745-6


*Chapter 3*

# EU-U.S. ECONOMIC TIES: FRAMEWORK, SCOPE AND MAGNITUDE[1]

*William H. Cooper*

## SUMMARY

The United States and the European Union (EU) economic relationship is the largest in the world—and it is growing. The modern U.S.-European economic relationship has evolved since World War II, broadening as the six-member European Community expanded into the present 27-member European Union. The ties have also become more complex and interdependent, covering a growing number and type of trade and financial activities

In 2009, $1,252.0 billion flowed between the United States and the EU on the current account, the most comprehensive measure of U.S. trade flows. The EU as a unit is the largest merchandise trading partner of the United States. In 2009, the EU accounted for $220.6 billion of total U.S. exports (or 20.8%) and for $281.8 billion of total U.S. imports (or 18.1%) for a U.S. trade deficit of $73.2 billion. The EU is also the largest U.S. trade partner when trade in services is added to trade in merchandise, accounting for $173.5 billion (or 34.5% of the total in U.S. services exports) and $134.8 billion (or 36.4% of

---

[1] [1] This is an edit, reformatted and augmented version of the Congressional Research Service Report for Congress RL30608.

total U.S. services imports) in 2009. In addition, in 2009, a net $114.1 billion *flowed* from U.S. residents to EU countries into direct investments, while a net $82.7 billion *flowed* from EU residents to direct investments in the United States.

Policy disputes arise between the United States and the EU generating tensions which sometimes lead to bilateral trade disputes. Yet, in spite of these disputes, the U.S.-EU economic relationship remains dynamic. It is a relationship that is likely to grow in importance assuming the trends toward globalization and the enlargement of the EU continue, forcing more trade and investment barriers to fall. Economists indicate that an expanded relationship would bring economic benefits to both sides in the form of wider choices of goods and services and greater investment opportunities.

But increasing economic interdependence brings challenges as well as benefits. As the U.S. and EU economies continue to integrate, some sectors or firms will "lose out" to increased competition and will resist the forces of change. Greater economic integration also challenges long-held notions of "sovereignty," as national or regional policies have extraterritorial impact. Similarly, accepted understanding of "competition," "markets," and other economic concepts are tested as national borders dissolve with closer integration of economies.

U.S. and EU policymakers are likely to face the task of how to manage the increasingly complex bilateral economic relationship in ways that maximize benefits and keep frictions to a minimum, including developing new frameworks. For members during the 112th Congress, it could mean weighing the benefits of greater economic integration against the costs to constituents in the context of overall U.S. national interests.

The bilateral economic relationship between the United States and the European Union (EU) is the largest such relationship in the world—and it is growing.[1] It is a relationship forged over several centuries, since the European colonization of North America.

The modern U.S.-European economic relationship has evolved since World War II. It has broadened as the six-member European Community expanded into the present 27-member European Union. The ties have also become more complex, covering a growing number and type of trade and financial activities that intertwine the economies on both sides of the Atlantic into an increasingly interdependent relationship. For members of Congress and other policymakers, the EU remains a significant participant in the U.S. economy and a major factor in policy considerations. For example, the EU and its members are influential members of the World Trade Organization (WTO), the Organization for Economic Cooperation and Development (OECD), the International Monetary Fund (IMF) and the World Bank. These countries, together with the United States, play decisive roles in developing and implementing the missions of those institutions.

Despite the tightness of the bilateral relationship, policy tensions arise generating tensions within the relationship, sometimes leading to bilateral trade disputes. The issues that arise are becoming more complex, reflecting the growing integration of the U.S. and EU economies. Yet, in spite of these disputes, the U.S.-EU economic relationship remains dynamic and one within which trillions of dollars of economic activity transpire.

This report provides background information and analysis of the U.S.-EU economic relationship for members of the 112th Congress as they contemplate the costs and benefits of closer U.S. economic ties with the EU. It examines the economic and political framework of the relationship and the scope and magnitude of the ties based on data from various sources. In addition, the report analyzes the implications these factors have for U.S. economic policy toward the EU. The report will be revised as events warrant.

## U.S. INTERESTS

The United States has been a strong advocate for the construction of close economic ties among the West European countries since the end of World War II. During the Cold War, the European Community served U.S. foreign policy and national security interests as a force of stability that drew former enemies—(West) Germany and France—closer together and that helped to build Western Europe into an economic bulwark against the Soviet Bloc.

The formation of an economically unified Europe has served U.S. economic interests as well by accelerating European economic growth and development which has opened trade and investment opportunities for the United States. Many studies have concluded that the formation of the EU has had a net positive economic impact on the world as a whole because it has led on balance to more trade *creation* than *diversion* of trade from other countries.

The EU continues to become a more closely knit entity with the formation of the European Monetary Union comprising 17 of the 27 members of the EU and their adoption of a common currency, the euro. These developments have already had an impact on U.S.-EU trade ties.

# The Framework of U.S.-EU Economic Ties

U.S.-EU economic relations exist within a framework of economic, political and security factors. Some of these factors have promoted closer economic relationships, while others have created tensions that have, at times, threatened to undermine the relationship.

The U.S.-EU economic relationship dominates the world economy by the sheer size of their combined economies. The combined population of United States and the EU members approaches 800 million people who generate a combined gross domestic product (GDP) that is roughly equivalent to 40% of world GDP in 2010.[2] Combined EU and U.S. world trade accounts for over 47% of all world trade. In other words, the U.S.-EU economic relationship has clout.

The United States and the EU member countries are of roughly equivalent levels of economic development and are among the most advanced in the world. As a group they include the world's wealthiest and most educated populations. The United States and the members of the EU, with a few exceptions, are major producers of advanced technologies and services. As a result U.S.-EU trade tends to be intra-industry trade; that is trade in similar products, such as cars and computers, dominate two-way trade flows. Furthermore, the United States and the EU have advanced and integrated financial sectors which facilitate large volumes of capital flows across the Atlantic. These capital flows account for a significant portion of the bilateral economic activity.

The dominance of security and defense matters is another factor influencing U.S.-EU ties. Twenty-one of the EU-27 are members of NATO, and represent an overwhelming majority of NATO's 26 members. NATO members must deal with a number of issues that pertain to foreign trade, such as defense-related government procurement, product standardization, controls of exports of dual-use technologies and related products, and economic sanctions. National security and foreign policy concerns strongly dominated the U.S.-European relationship during the Cold War.[3]

The 153-member WTO (and its predecessor, the General Agreement on Tariffs and Trade (GATT)) is a critical part of the EU-U.S. bilateral economic framework. The WTO provides the principles and rules under which the U.S. and the EU conduct much of their trade. The basic principles of most-favored-nation(MFN), or nondiscriminatory, treatment and of national treatment of imports of goods and services and of foreign investments, along with WTO rules on trade-related intellectual property rights, investment, and trade remedy practices (antidumping and countervailing duties and safeguards) are the foundation of U.S. and European trade and investment policies. The WTO also provides the mechanism by which the United States and the EU resolve many of their bilateral trade disputes.

To a lesser extent, the OECD is an important element in the U.S.-EU framework. Largely consisting of fully industrialized countries, the 34-member OECD coordinates economic policies and reviews economic conditions and polices of its members and those of some non-members. The OECD also has some rules and guidelines for trade and investment practices of its members. For example, the OECD Arrangement on Official Export Credits curbs the subsidization of exports.

EU and U.S. policies and practices form another element of the bilateral economic framework. The United States and the EU share a commitment to open trade and investment. The United States and European countries were largely instrumental in establishing the post-World War II foundation for an open international economic system. This commitment has played a large role in the strong economic ties between them. Yet, the two sides differ in some significant policy areas, for example, the EU's Common Agricultural Policy, conflicting competition policies, and the U.S. extraterritorial application of economic sanctions against Cuba and other countries. These policy differences have been a source of significant bitterness and controversy.

## U.S.-EU Trade in Goods and Services

The EU as a unit is the largest merchandise trading partner of the United States. In 2009, the EU accounted for $220.6 billion of total U.S. exports (or 20.8%) and for $281.8 billion of total U.S. imports (or 18.1%) for a U.S. trade deficit of $73.2 billion. At the same time, the United States is the largest non-EU trading partner of the EU as a whole. In 2009, EU exports to the United States accounted for 18.3% of total exports to non-EU countries, while EU imports from the United States accounted for 12.9% of total imports from non-EU countries.[4]

For a number of years, the United States realized trade surpluses with the EU. However, since 1993, the United States has been incurring growing trade deficits with the EU ($73.2 billion in 2009). Economists attribute the growth in the U.S. trade deficit with the EU to, among other factors, differences in U.S. and economic growth rates and the weakening of the dollar compared to the euro.

**Table 1. U.S. Merchandise Trade with Selected Trade Partners, 2009 (billions of dollars)**

| Partner | U.S. Exports | U.S. Imports | U.S. Trade Turnover | U.S. Trade Balances |
|---|---|---|---|---|
| EU-27 | 220.6 | 281.8 | 502.4 | -73.2 |
| Canada | 204.7 | 226.2 | 430.9 | -21.6 |
| Mexico | 151.5 | 215.9 | 347.3 | -74.6 |
| China | 71.5 | 337.8 | 386.8 | -266.3 |
| Japan | 51.1 | 95.8 | 146.9 | -44.7 |
| World | 1,056.0 | 1,559.6 | 2,615.6 | -503.6 |

Source: U.S. Department of Commerce. Bureau of the Census.

Among the top U.S. exports to the EU have been aircraft, and machinery of various kinds, including computers, integrated circuits, and office machine parts. A large share of U.S. imports from the EU has consisted of passenger cars, machinery of various types, including gas turbines, computers and components, office machinery, and parts and organic chemicals. Within the EU, Germany, the United Kingdom, and France are the leading U.S. trading partners, followed by the Netherlands and Italy.

The EU is the largest U.S. trade partner when trade in services is added to trade in merchandise. In 2009 the EU accounted for $173.5 billion (or 34.5% of the total in U.S. services exports). Of this amount, $26.7 billion derived from receipts for various travel services, $7.8 billion from payments for passenger fares, and $12.0 billion for other transportation fees (freight and port services). Another $40.7 billion were in receipts for royalties and licensing fees and $84.6 billion derived from other private sector services, including business, professional and technical services (including legal services), and insurance. Also included under services are revenues from transfers under U.S. military contracts which equaled $1.3 billion in 2009.

In 2009, the EU accounted for $134.8 billion (or 36.4% of total U.S. services imports)—including travel services ($18.5 billion), passenger fees ($10.7 billion), and freight and port fees ($14.5 billion). Royalties and licensing fees accounted for another $14.7 billion. In addition, other private sector services accounted for $63.0 billion of imports. Also included were payments of $11.9 billion in defense-related expenditures.[5]

**Table 2. U.S. Trade with the European Union in Goods and Services, 1999-2009 (billions of dollars)**

| | 1999 | 2000 | 2001 | 2002 | 2003 | 2004 | 2005 | 2006 | 2007 | 2008 | 2009 |
|---|---|---|---|---|---|---|---|---|---|---|---|
| Goods & Services | 236.4 | 257.5 | 244.5 | 238.4 | 250.7 | 283.2 | 314.3 | 353.5 | 424.7 | 472.4 | 398.0 |
| Goods[a] | 148.9 | 162.3 | 155.8 | 140.4 | 147.6 | 167.6 | 183.4 | 210.2 | 242.2 | 275.9 | 224.5 |
| Services | 87.6 | 95.2 | 88.7 | 98.0 | 103.2 | 115.6 | 130.8 | 143.3 | 182.5 | 196.5 | 173.5 |
| | **1999** | **2000** | **2001** | **2002** | **2003** | **2004** | **2005** | **2006** | **2007** | **2008** | **2009** |
| Goods & Services | 264.4 | 298.6 | 293.2 | 311.3 | 338.6 | 387.6 | 427.3 | 459.4 | 502.0 | 525.9 | 419.2 |
| Goods[a] | 194.5 | 219.9 | 219.5 | 225.4 | 244.9 | 278.9 | 309.0 | 330.4 | 356.2 | 374.4 | 284.4 |
| Services | 69.9 | 78.7 | 73.7 | 85.2 | 93.7 | 108.7 | 118.3 | 129.0 | 145.8 | 151.6 | 134.8 |
| | **1999** | **2000** | **2001** | **2002** | **2003** | **2004** | **2005** | **2006** | **2007** | **2008** | **2009** |
| Goods & Services | -28.0 | -41.1 | -48.7 | -72.9 | -87.8 | -104.4 | -113.0 | -105.9 | -77.2 | -53.5 | -21.2 |
| Goods[a] | -45.6 | -57.6 | -63.7 | -85.0 | -97.3 | -111.3 | -125.5 | -120.2 | -113.9 | -98.5 | -59.9 |
| Services | 17.7 | 16.5 | 15.0 | 9.7 | 9.5 | 6.9 | 12.5 | 14.3 | 36.7 | 45.0 | 38.6 |

a. The figures for goods trade while essentially equivalent to those for merchandise trade in Table 1 are slightly lower as they are measured on a balance of payments basis, rather than a census basis. 2009 figures are preliminary and subject to revision.

Source: U.S. Department of Commerce. Bureau of Economic Analysis. *Survey of Current Business*. Various issues.

**Table 3. U.S. Current Account Balance with EU, 2009 (billions of dollars)**

| | |
|---|---|
| Exports Goods and Services | 398.0 |
| Imports Goods and Services | 419.2 |
| Income Receipts | 239.5 |
| Income Payments | 190.7 |
| Unilateral Transfers (Net) | 4.6 |
| **Total Current Account Flows** | **1252.0** |
| **Current Account Balance** | **22.9** |

Source: U.S. Department of Commerce. Bureau of Economic Analysis. *U.S. International Transactions Accounts Data* June 29,2010. http://www.bea.gov Data are preliminary and subject to revision.

Table 2 indicates that the United States has consistently run surpluses in services trade with the EU. These surpluses helped, albeit modestly, to offset the U.S. merchandise trade deficits.

A substantial amount of funds flows between the United States and the EU as receipts of income derived from assets, including direct and portfolio investments and government securities. In 2009, $239.5 billion flowed to the United States from income earned on EU assets held by U.S. residents. In 2009, $190.7 billion flowed to the EU as income earned on assets held in the United States by EU residents. In addition, a net $4.6 billion flowed into the United States as unilateral transfers. Trade in goods and services, plus income receipts and payments, plus unilateral transfers, make up the U.S. current account, the most comprehensive measure of U.S. trade flows. In 2009, the United States incurred a current account surplus with the EU of $22.9 billion.[6]

In sum, the flows of merchandise or goods trade, services trade, and income between the United States and the EU manifest a very active, strong, and large economic relationship. In 2009 alone, a total of more than $1252.0 billion flowed between the United States and the EU.[7]

## U.S.-EU Investment Flows and Positions

Transactions on the current account represented only a part of the volume of international financial *flows* between the United States and EU in 2009. The remaining transactions are on the *capital account* which derive from payments by the U.S. government and residents to obtain assets in the EU and by EU residents to obtain assets in the United States.[8] These assets include government purchases of gold and foreign currencies for their official reserves and government purchases of other foreign assets. The capital account also includes payments by U.S. residents for portfolio investments (including bank deposits, government securities, corporate stocks, and bonds, and other private sector securities) and payments to obtain direct investments (including real estate, plants, factories, and commercial establishments). In 2009, because of the global recession, U.S. investors on a net basis, repatriated from the EU $15.4 billion dollars, and EU investors on a net basis repatriated $155.8 billion in order to shore up their domestic capital bases.[9]

Foreign direct investments (FDI) represent long-term commitments on the part of the investor. In 2009, a net $114.1 billion *flowed* from U.S. residents to EU countries into direct investments, while a net $82.7 billion *flowed* from EU residents to direct investments in the United States.[10] By the end of 2009, the *position* of U.S. direct investment in EU countries stood at $1,733.8 billion, or 49.4% of all foreign direct investment by U.S. residents.[11] Of that total, $250.1 billion, or 14.4%, was in the manufacturing sector. Another 24.2% was in banking and other financial establishments, and insurance firms. The Netherlands and the United Kingdom, the largest targets, each accounted for 27.2%. At the end of 2009, EU residents had foreign direct investments in the United States valued at $1,475.1 billion, or 63.6% of total foreign direct investments in the United States. The United Kingdom was the largest source of those investments with 19.6% of the total in 2009.[12]

## CONCLUSIONS AND POLICY IMPLICATIONS

Foreign trade and investment data depict a strong, interdependent, and significant U.S.-EU bilateral economic relationship. It is a relationship that is likely to grow in importance as advancements in technology and other forces of globalization, plus the future enlargement of the EU, force more trade and investment barriers to fall. The expanded relationship is widely seen as bringing economic benefits to both sides in the form of wider choices of goods and services and greater investment opportunities.

But increasing economic interdependence brings challenges as well as benefits. U.S.-EU trade ties have been plagued by disputes that at times have reached the highest levels of policymaking. While these disputes have covered a range of sectors and issues, the most contentious and public have been related to trade in agricultural and agricultural-related products. The United

States has taken the EU to task for its ban on hormone-enhanced beef imports and for its policy regarding banana imports.

Yet, the agriculture sector accounts for a very small portion of not only U.S.-EU bilateral trade but also for the total world trade of the two entities. In 2009, agriculture accounted for 3.4 % of total U.S. exports to the EU and for 3.9 % of total imports from the EU.[13] It is beyond the scope of this report to analyze this contrast between U.S. and EU trade policies and trade volume. But the contrast suggests that the attention received by these disputes at the official level, as well as from the press, reflects the domestic political salience of these issues to a much further extent than their overall commercial or economic significance.

Greater economic integration also challenges long-held notions of "sovereignty," as national or regional policies have extraterritorial impact. For example, the U.S. use of foreign policy trade sanctions against such "rogue states" as Cuba and Iran affected EU firms and investors and caused sharp U.S.-EU friction. Similarly, accepted understandings of "competition," "markets," and other economic concepts are tested as national borders dissolve with closer integration of economies.

U.S. and EU policymakers, therefore, continually face the task of how to manage the increasingly complex bilateral economic relationship in ways that maximize benefits and keep frictions to a minimum. For members of Congress it means weighing the benefits and costs to constituents of greater economic integration and placing this calculation in the context of overall U.S. national interests.

## End Notes

[1] The EU consists of Austria, Belgium, Bulgaria, Cyprus (Greek), Czech Republic, Denmark, Estonia, Finland, France, Germany, Greece, Hungary, Ireland, Italy, Latvia, Lithuania, Luxembourg, Malta, Netherlands, Poland, Portugal, Romania ,Slovakia, Slovenia, Spain, Sweden, and the United Kingdom.

[2] CIA. *World Factbook.* 2010. https://www.cia.gov/

[3] But even the dominance of national security concerns did not prevent at least some major disputes to surface between the United States and the EU. For example, in June 1982, the United States imposed controls on exports to the Soviet Union of oil and gas equipment technology that was produced by U.S.-owned firms in foreign countries. The restrictions were in response to Soviet support of martial law in Poland and to hamper the construction of a natural gas pipeline that would deliver Soviet gas to Western Europe. The measures led to an open confrontation with the European Community which argued that the United States could not apply U.S. controls outside the United States. The United States rescinded the controls in November 1982. Featherstone, Kevin and Roy H. Ginsburg. *The United States*

*and the European Community in the 1990s: Partners in Transition.* St. Martin's Press. United Kingdom. 1993. p. 179-180.

[4] Calculations for U.S. trade based on data from the U.S. Department of Commerce. Bureau of the Census. EU trade data from Eurostat. Both sets of data were compiled by Global Trade Information Systems, Inc. as part of World Trade Atlas.

[5] U.S. Department of Commerce. Bureau of Economic Analysis. *U.S. International Transactions Accounts Data.* June 29, 2010.

[6] U.S. Department of Commerce. Bureau of Economic Analysis. *U.S. International Transactions Accounts Data.* June 29, 2010. http://www.bea.gov

[7] Ibid.

[8] The Department of Commerce only reports net, rather than total, capital inflows and outflows. The capital account is also the mirror image of the current account in U.S. balance of payments accounts.

[9] U.S. Department of Commerce. Bureau of Economic Analysis. http://www.bea.gov. June 29, 2010.

[10] Ibid.

[11] The foreign investment *position* represents the value of total accumulated investments in place and is valued on an historical-cost basis, that is, the value at the time of purchase. Foreign investment *flows* represent the net value of investment transaction during a particular year.

[12] U.S. Department of Commerce. Bureau of Economic Analysis. *Survey of Current Business.* July 2009. p. 13,15.

[13] Calculations made on data obtained from United States International Trade Commission dataweb June 30, 2010.

In: U.S.- EU Regulatory Cooperation
Editor: William C. Ahrens

ISBN: 978-1-62100-745-6


*Chapter 4*

# U.S.-EU TRADE AND ECONOMIC RELATIONS: KEY POLICY ISSUES FOR THE 112th CONGRESS[1]

***Raymond J. Ahearn***

## SUMMARY

The 112th Congress, in both its legislative and oversight roles, will confront numerous issues that affect the trade and economic relationship between the United States and the European Union (EU). As U. S. -EU commercial interactions drive significant job creation on both sides of the Atlantic, Congress can be expected to monitor ongoing efforts to deepen transatlantic ties that are already large, dynamic, and mutually beneficial.

U.S. and European private stakeholders, concerned about slow growth, job creation, and increased competition from emerging economies, have urged Brussels and Washington to strengthen transatlantic trade and economic ties by reducing or eliminating remaining trade barriers and by cooperating more closely in addressing global economic challenges. A select group of these issues are examined in this report.

Three proposals for deepening the transatlantic marketplace are the reduction of regulatory barriers, the negotiation of a zero-tariff agreement, and

---

[1] This is an edit, reformatted and augmented version of the Congressional Research Service Report for Congress R41652.

movement towards a barrier-free investment environment. Under the auspices of the Transatlantic Economic Council (TEC), the reduction of regulatory barriers is the approach being most actively pursued by U. S. and European policymakers.

At the last TEC meeting, held in December 2010, the two sides agreed to focus on aligning regulations in emerging technologies, such as nanotechnology or electric cars, before laws or regulations have been promulgated. Previous efforts to harmonize regulations on a sector-by-sector basis proved difficult due to bureaucratic resistance. Whether the TEC will realize its potential as a mechanism to accelerate the integration of the U. S. -EU market remains to be seen.

Despite generally low tariff levels on both sides, some in the U. S. and EU business communities support negotiating the elimination of all remaining tariffs imposed on U. S. -EU trade through a bilateral negotiation. Support for a zero-tariff agreement is based on a combination of factors, including the agreement's ability to generate economic benefits for both sides and the leverage such an agreement could create for pressuring emerging economies to make more concessions in the Doha Round of multilateral trade negotiations.

Greater collaboration and alignment of U. S. and EU approaches towards addressing global economic challenges, such as completing the Doha Round, dealing with China's trade barriers, and reducing global imbalances, remain a work in progress. Given shared interests in opening emerging markets further to industrial goods and services, business interests have urged U. S. and EU negotiators to work more closely together to press other countries for more concessions. EU negotiators in the past have remained reluctant to move in this direction perhaps out of concern that greater ambition would require further EU concessions on agriculture.

According to some, closer U. S.-EU cooperation in addressing problems posed by China's interventionist policies could facilitate pragmatic solutions and successful outcomes if China's leaders understood there was no distance between U. S. and EU positions. In this view, a divided U. S. -EU economic policy approach to China could allow it to play one side off against the other.

On the question of reducing global trade imbalances, the two sides appear far apart. Influenced by German insistence on fiscal austerity, Europe's trade and current account balance could increase greatly in the coming years, thereby making it much more difficult to reduce global imbalances.

## INTRODUCTION

The United States and the European Union (EU) share a large, dynamic, and mutually beneficial economic relationship. Not only are trade and investment ties between the two partners huge in absolute terms, but the relative importance of bilateral trade and investment flows for each partner has remained high and relatively constant over time, despite the rise of China and other Asian economies. [1]

The EU as a bloc is the United States' largest trade and investment partner by a large margin. As shown in Table 1, the EU accounted for 23% of U. S. merchandise trade in goods and services in 2009. Canada, the second largest trading partner, accounted for 14% of total U. S. trade in goods and services.

The importance of the EU is even greater on the foreign direct investment side, where European companies accounted for $1. 5 trillion, or 63%, of total foreign direct investment in the United States and U. S. companies accounted for $1. 7 trillion, or about 50%, of total foreign investment in Europe in 2009. These investments account for four million workers on both sides of the Atlantic being directly employed by the respective affiliates of U. S. or European-based companies. The German company Siemens, for example, employs some 60,000 people in the United States and General Electric employs some 70,000 workers in Europe. [2]

**Table 1. U.S. Trade in Goods and Services with Top Five Partners, 2009 (billions of U.S. dollars)**

| Partner | U.S. Exports | U.S. Imports | Trade Turnover | % of U.S. Trade |
|---|---|---|---|---|
| EU-27 | 379 | 419 | 817 | 23 |
| Canada | 248 | 251 | 499 | 14 |
| China | 86 | 305 | 391 | 11 |
| Mexico | 152 | 193 | 345 | 10 |
| Japan | 94 | 120 | 214 | 6 |
| World | 1,571 | 1,946 | 3,517 | 100 |

Source: U. S. Department of Commerce, Bureau of Economic Analysis; *U. S. International Accounts Data;* http://www. bea. gov.

Notes: Trade turnover is the sum of U. S. exports and imports.

The U.S. -EU trade and investment relationship, what many call the transatlantic economy, is not only the largest in the world, but also arguably the most important because of its sheer size. As shown in Table 2, the flows of merchandise or goods trade, services trade, and income across the Atlantic manifest a very active, strong, and large economic relationship. In 2009 alone, a total of$1,247 billion flowed between the United States and the EU, or an average of $3. 4 billion per day.

With a combined population slightly over 818 million or about 12% of the world's population, the two partners produce around 50 percent of the world's GDP. Combined with bilateral trade flows in goods and services that account for 40% of the world total, the magnitude of transatlantic economic transactions means that the two sides have significant influence and leadership responsibilities in the world economy. Agreement and cooperation between the two partners in the past has been critical to making the global trading system more open and efficient.

The high degree of transatlantic economic interdependence, however, carries some downside risks, as demonstrated by the 2008 financial crisis, which started in the United States and was then transmitted to Europe. As the U. S. economy is now recovering from the deep recession, EU members Greece, Ireland, Portugal, and Spain are struggling to address sovereign debt crises which are slowing Europe's economic growth and recovery. With a significant stake in European economic growth, there is a concern that U. S. exports may be adversely affected at a time when the Obama Administration hopes to double US. exports by 2015. [3]

Given the magnitude of commercial interaction, trade disputes are not unexpected. Policymakers tend to maintain that the United States and the EU always have more in common than in dispute, and like to point out that trade disputes usually affect a small fraction (often estimated at 1-2 percent) of trade in goods and services. Both sides have been working to resolve some of the biggest disputes for years. These include a dispute between the aerospace manufacturers, Airbus and Boeing, and conflicts over bio-engineered food products and protection of geographical indicators. The Airbus-Boeing dispute involves allegations of unfair subsidization for both companies and is being adjudicated by the World Trade Organization dispute resolution process. The agricultural-based disputes are rooted in different approaches to regulation, as well as different social preferences.

U.S. -EU trade and economic relations are also characterized by other forms of competition andrivalry. Each side aspires to lead in setting rules for global trade and investment, often in an effort intended to facilitate commercial success for its respective companies. Similarly, both economic powers often compete to secure bilateral and regional trade agreements to support jobs, markets, and foreign policy interests. No where may this be more apparent than in the EU's rush to negotiate a free trade agreement with South Korea following the negotiation of the U.S.-South Korean FTA in 2007.[4]

**Table 2. U.S. Current Account Balance with the EU, 2009 (billions of U.S. dollars)**

| Transactions | Totals |
|---|---|
| U. S. Exports of Goods and Services | 397. 9 |
| U. S. Imports of Goods and Services | 419. 2 |
| U. S. Income Receipts (derived from U. S. assets,including direct and portfolio investments and government securities) | 239. 5 |
| U. S Income Payments (derived from EU assets,including direct and portfolio investments and government securities) | 190. 7 |
| Total Current Account Flows | 1,247. 3 |
| Daily average flow based on the current account | 3. 4 |

Source: U. S. Department of Commerce, Bureau of Economic Analysis; *U. S. International Transactions Accounts Data;* February 14, 2010. http://www. bea. gov.

Notes: The current account is the most comprehensive measure of U. S. international trade and financial transactions with the world. Net unilateral transfers (government grants, pensions, and private remittances) totaling -$4. 6 billion are not included in this table.

While the U.S. and EU economies are very open to trade and investment flows from both sides, some barriers to trade and investment remain. Various studies, in fact, estimate that substantial economic gains in terms of jobs and faster growth could be attained if progress was made in reducing a range of remaining tariff barriers at the border and regulatory "behind the border" non-tariff barriers.[5]

Private stakeholders on both sides have urged policymakers to cooperate more closely to reduce remaining barriers to trade and to provide greater leadership for the world economy. Such actions, stakeholders argue, are a way to boost transatlantic economic growth and jobs.[6] Cooperation is said to be particularly important given that global economic wealth and political power is shifting towards emerging economies such as China, India, and Brazil. While these developing countries are providing new sources of economic growth, they have different views on the future direction of the world economy. This could create a need for greater U.S.-EU cooperation in addressing global challenges that are important for job creation and growth for both sides.

The 112th Congress, in both its legislative and oversight roles, could face numerous issues that affect the U.S-EU trade and economic relationship. A select group of these issues are identified and briefly described in this report. The issues are grouped into two categories:

- those concerning efforts to deepen U.S.-EU economic ties; and
- those that involve efforts to strengthen the global economy.

As these issues cut across trade, economic, regulatory, and foreign policy subject matters, a number of congressional committees may have legislative or oversight responsibilities in whole or in part. On the House side, these include the Committees on Agriculture, Energy and Commerce, Financial Services, Foreign Affairs, Judiciary, Transportation and Infrastructure, and Ways and Means. On the Senate side, these include the Committees on Agriculture, Banking, Commerce, Science, and Transportation, Energy and Natural Resources, Environment and Public Works, Finance, Foreign Relations, and Judiciary.

# DEEPENING TRANSATLANTIC ECONOMIC TIES

Proposals for deepening transatlantic economic ties include the reduction of regulatory barriers, the negotiation of a zero tariff agreement, and movement towards a barrier-free investment environment. Each proposal holds the prospect of producing economic gains in terms of jobs and growth for both sides, but each also faces obstacles as freer trade creates winners and losers when it comes to jobs. Currently, the reduction of regulatory barriers is the one approach that is being actively pursued.

## Reducing Regulatory Barriers

Since the mid-1990s, both U. S. and European multinational companies (MNCs) have consistently identified divergent regulatory frameworks for both goods and services as the most serious barriers to transatlantic commerce. Redundant standards, testing, and certification procedures are seen by these companies as far more costly and harmful than any trade barriers imposed at the border, such as tariffs or quotas. While the purpose of many regulations is to protect consumers and the environment, divergent domestic regulations and standards add to the cost of doing business on both sides of the Atlantic and serve as non-tariff barriers to trade in many different economic activities and sectors. By reducing gaps in regulatory policies and standards, the United States and EU hope to benefit thousands of companies engaged in transatlantic trade by reducing costs, streamlining time-to-market, and improving competitiveness vis-à-vis third countries. [7]

A 2009 study commissioned by the European Commission estimated that aligning and rationalizing these kinds of non-tariff barriers would bring its economy potential gains of $158 billion in annual GDP and increase exports to the United States by 2%. EU sectors that stand to benefit include motor vehicles, chemicals, pharmaceuticals, food, and electrical goods. The United States, it was estimated, stands to gain some $53 billion in annual GDP and a 6% increase in annual exports to the EU, with the primary beneficiaries being sectors such as electrical goods, chemicals, pharmaceuticals, financial services, and insurance.[8]

Many efforts have been made over the past 15 years to tackle and reduce these behind-the-border regulatory barriers, but with only limited success.[9] Predicated on the notion that past initiatives failed to make significant progress in enhancing regulatory progress, the Transatlantic Economic Council (TEC) was established in April 2007 at the U.S. -EU Summit. Created as a new entity by German Chancellor Angela Merkel (then European Council President), European Commission President Manuel Barroso, and President George W. Bush, the TEC was designed to provide minister-level political guidance (headed on both sides by Cabinet/Ministerial-level appointees) to foster regulatory cooperation and to reduce or eliminate regulatory burdens to trade. The TECalso covers issues such as investment, innovation, intellectual property rights, secure trade, and financial markets. The ultimate aim of the TEC is to create an integrated transatlantic market.

The Summit leaders also created an advisory group to the TEC and invited the U. S. Congress, along with the European Parliament, to accept a new, more substantive role in transatlantic regulatory cooperation by becoming part of the advisory group. In short, the TEC was designed to deal with some of the perceived shortcomings of previous transatlantic regulatory initiatives by providing high level political leadership, more involvement of legislators and other stakeholders in the regulatory process, and a greater emphasis on results than process. [10]

In the first three years (2007-2009) of its now almost four year history, the TEC was used primarily as a mechanism to try to resolve a number of longstanding bilateral trade disputes, most notably the EU's ban on imports of poultry that has been washed in chlorine. Efforts to harmonize regulations on a sector-by-sector basis also proved difficult due to political and bureaucratic resistance on both sides to revise existing laws and regulations. But in late 2010 the two sides agreed to focus future efforts substantially on aligning regulations and standards in emerging or new technologies, such as nanotechnology or electric cars, well before laws or regulations have been promulgated. Accordingly, at their fifth and most recent meeting, held in Washington on December 17, 2010, the TEC agreed to a work program focusing on sectors where regulatory cooperation can help avoid unintended trade barriers in the future.

Among the highlights of this latest TEC meeting, the two sides agreed to develop a process for implementing compatible approaches for the regulation of new and innovative sectors. In this manner, it is hoped that trade disputes due to different regulations could be avoided. The meeting also provided new impetus for regulatory cooperation in specific sectors such as electronic health records, energy-saving products, and electric vehicles as a way of reducing costs and preempting unnecessary obstacles to exports. The TEC meeting also launched an Innovation Action Plan designed to strengthen joint efforts to promote innovation and the commercialization of emerging technologies.[11]

These work plans were touted by senior officials as more specific and time-bound than previous work plans. Whether the results will be more tangible and commercially significant remains to be seen. Part of the problem is that regulatory cooperation is difficult and technically demanding work, with wide differences between the two sides concerning approaches to regulation. Key differences bear on public preferences and tolerance for risk, attitudes towards transparency, and institutional capacities to undertake regulatory reforms.[12]

## Negotiating a Zero-Tariff Agreement

When U.S. and EU trade officials meet these days, it is more likely that they will be discussing product standards and regulations than tariff barriers imposed at the border. One reason this is the case is that successive rounds of multilateral trade liberalization have dramatically reduced tariffs on transatlantic trade in goods, including food, to very low levels. In the United

States, the simple average tariff imposed on a most-favored-nation basis on imports of manufactured goods and agricultural products is around 4% and 9%, respectively. Comparable figures for the EU are 4% on manufactures and 18% on agricultural products.[13]

Despite these generally low average tariff levels, there is interest in the U.S. and EU business communities to eliminate all remaining tariffs imposed on U.S.-EU trade through a bilateral negotiation. Support for the proposal is based on a combination of factors, including the agreement's ability to: (1) generate economic benefits for both sides, including reducing costs to companies that pay tariffs on trade with their foreign affiliates; (2) re-energize transatlantic economic ties; and (3) pressure recalcitrant countries in the Doha Round to undertake more concessions. [14]

One recent study estimated that there would be significant trade and welfare benefits for both sides from a full elimination of tariffs on U.S.-EU merchandise trade over time.[15] In the aggregate, the study projects that total EU exports to the United States could increase by up to $69 billion in value, or 18 percent, while U. S. exports to the EU could rise by up to $53 billion, or 17 percent. In terms of increases in GDP, the EU economy could gain anywhere from $58 billion to $85 billion and the U. S. economy anywhere from $59 billion to $82 billion.[16] These potential gains, according to the authors, are considerable in absolute terms and higher than in most preferential free trade agreements signed by the United States or EU, or agreements currently being negotiated. [17]

In the past, a major objection to a transatlantic zero-tariff agreement was that it could undermine the multilateral system because it was a preferential or discriminatory trade agreement between the two biggest trade blocs in the world. Critics maintained that such an agreement would likely be inconsistent with the WTO obligation that preferential agreements cover "substantially all trade."[18] This is particularly due to strong opposition on both sides to include a number of agricultural sectors. [19] As a result, critics traditionally argue that any preferential agreement struck by the world's biggest economies would send a signal to the rest of the world that the United States and EU had abdicated responsibility for leadership of the multilateral system and could spell the death knell of efforts to bring the Doha Round to a close.

Supporters have countered that a zero-tariff agreement could cover "substantially all trade" in a WTO-consistent manner by exempting only a handful of sensitive agricultural products from tariff elimination on both sides and by providing long phase-out periods for tariff cuts on other sensitive agricultural items. Given the long stalemate in completing the Doha Round, supporters also view a U.S.-EU preferential agreement as creating new leverage for the United States and EU to use in an effort to influence emerging economies to make more constructive offers to conclude the Doha Round. They also point to past instances in which regional or bilateral agreements, such as NAFTA, may have served to spur multilateral trade liberalization. [20]

For the ObamaAdministration to enter into a tariff negotiation with the EU, Congress would have to extend the President's tariff-cutting authority. To date, no such proposals have been introduced in the 112th Congress.

## Negotiating a Barrier-Free Investment Agreement

Foreign investment has overtaken trade as the major component of U.S.-EU economic relations. While the two sides together account for around 40% of world trade in goods and services, they account for over 60% of the inward stock of foreign direct investment (FDI) and 75% of the outward stock of FDI. Moreover, Europe and the United States remain the most profitable regions of the world for each other's multinational corporations, accounting for about half of total global affiliate earnings. [21]

These high levels of cross-investment are facilitated by two of the most open and hospitable climates for foreign investment in the world. At the same time, pressures for investment protection have surfaced from time to time and some restrictions on foreign investment persist. [22]

European companies seeking to invest in the United States face two possible hurdles. The first are U.S. restrictions on foreign ownership in the shipping, energy, and communications sectors. The second relates to the review process the United States has established for examining foreign acquisitions, mergers, and takeovers from a national security perspective. [23] While this interagency process, known as the Committee on Foreign Investment in the United States (CFIUS), has generally run smoothly, the EU has raised concerns about the legal and economic costs for firms to circumvent or undergo CFIUS review. [24]

The EU position with regard to investment restrictions is more complicated than in the United States. The EU requires national treatment for foreign investors in most sectors and, with few exceptions, EU law requires that any company established under the laws of one member state must receive national treatment in all member states, regardless of a company's ownership. While EU law does impose some restrictions on foreign investment, member statesimpose arange of different policies and practices on foreign investors that are far more restrictive.[25]

Prior to the adoption of the Lisbon Treaty in December 2009, the European Commission shared competence with member states on investment issues.[26] Member states negotiated their own Bilateral Investment Treaties (BITs) and generally retained responsibility for their own investment regimes, while the EU negotiated investment provisions in EU preferential trade agreements.[27] Under Lisbon (Article 207), the competence for investment rests solely with the EU. However, foreign direct investment is not defined in the Treaty, leaving unclear the practical implications for EU efforts to negotiate investment agreements and set EU investment rules. If member states and the European Commission agree on a broad definition, the EU will have much greater authority on this issue and may be eager to enter into a major negotiation to demonstrate its new competence over investment policy. [28]

Calls for a U.S-EU investment agreement that would create a barrier-free climate for bilateral investment and serve as a model for the rest of the world are not new. In the past, some have proposed that agreement could be modeled on the current bilateral investment treaties, with a dispute resolution process that would allow foreign investors and host governments to address their differences. The accord could also establish minimal standards for corporate governance and transparency designed to ensure that the host country has reasonable confidence in the identity and management of the investing company, as well as include new issues such as e-commerce, competition policy, and limits on the use of local (sub-federal) investment incentives. Once an accord was in place, foreign investors would be able to invest in all sectors of the economy, with exceptions only for national security. [29]

Any attempt to harmonize processes for considering national security exceptions would likely be very difficult. While the U.S. CFIUS process has been in place for many years, there is no similar overarching framework in Europe that allows for security considerations to be balanced against commercial interests in a systematic way. Arguably, a great diversity of attitudes towards foreign investment throughout Europe could make it difficult to develop an EU-wide approach. [30]

## Cooperation to Strengthen the World Economy

For much of the post World War II era, the United States and Europe provided key leadership to the global economy. Given the heft of their combined economies, what was decided by the two powers was often adopted by the rest of the world. While the United States and the EU still today remain central to the global economy, other countries have grown in prominence. This redistribution of global economic power, in turn, arguably increases the need for the United States and EU to work together to promote their continued competitiveness, and to ensure that the rules of the global economy remain steeped in values and principles that both sides share.

Such cooperation is already taking place on a wide range of issues including access to raw materials, intellectual property protection, and changes in global and financial market governance. This section highlights mutual challenges on completing the Doha Round, influencing China to operate its economy more in accord with market principles, and reducing global imbalances.

## Completing the Doha Round of Multilateral Trade Negotiations

The United States and the EU have played a special role in creating the post-war WWII global trade and finance framework of market-based rules and institutions. The relative openness of the world trading system has been greatly facilitated by multilateral negotiations and agreements undertaken under the auspices of the General Agreement on Tariffs and Trade (GATT) and now its successor organization, the World Trade Organization (WTO). Yet, the WTO Doha Development Round of multilateral trade negotiations, begun in November 2001, has entered its 10$^{th}$ year, making it the longest running multilateral negotiation in the postwar era. While the last multilateral trade negotiation, the Uruguay Round, took eight years to complete (1986 to 1994), many observers believe that a Doha agreement needs to be reached this year to boost global trade, create jobs, bolster economic confidence, and maintain the credibility of the multilateral process. [31]

The Doha negotiations have been characterized by persistent differences between developed and developing countries on major issues affecting agriculture, industrial tariffs and non-tariff barriers, and services. The United States and the EU, for the most part, have shared similar interests in encouraging developing countries, particularly the big emerging economies such as China, Brazil, and India, to open their markets further for services and manufactured goods, while retaining some measure of protection for their own agricultural sectors. [32] Developing countries have sought the reduction of U.S. and EU agricultural tariffs and subsidies, non-reciprocal market access for manufacturing sectors, and protection for their services industries. Because U.S. and EU markets are already quite open, developing countries may not believe that they have much to gain by giving up protection of their markets for goods and services. Some developing countries also may fear that additional concessions may lead to greater competition from China rather than the United States or Europe.[33]

Despite a strong coincidence of interests, some distance between the U.S. and EU positions developed over a July 2008 draft agreement that was proposed in Geneva. EU trade officials viewed the draft as a possible basis for an agreement, but U.S. trade officials, backed by U.S. business and farm lobbies, argued that the concessions offered by the emerging economies were too minimal to form the basis for a deal. As a result, subsequent efforts have been made by the United States to persuade China, Brazil, and India to provide more trade and investment liberalization without much active assistance from EU negotiators.[34]

Given shared interests in opening emerging markets further to industrial goods and services, U.S. and some EU business interests have urged negotiators on both sides to work together to more actively press these other economies for concessions. EU negotiators have remained skeptical and somewhat reluctant to move in this direction perhaps out of concern that greater ambition would require further EU concessions on agriculture.[35]

It remains uncertain whether closer U.S.-EU cooperation and coordination in pushing developing countries to make additional concessions would be successful. However, if a more ambitious Doha agreement is not struck by the end of 2011, many observers believe that it could result in the first outright failure of a multilateral trade round in the postwar era. What impact this might have on the multilateral trading system and the WTO's credibility as a negotiating forum and as an arbitrator of trade disputes remains to be seen. But such an outcome could leave the United States and the EU with the challenge of developing other approaches for liberalizing trade on a multilateral basis and for strengthening the WTO as an institution.

## Dealing with China

China presents major trade challenges and opportunities for both the United States and the EU. Three decades ago, China's trade with the United States and the EU was negligible. Today China is the EU's second largest trade partner, after the United States, and its biggest source of imports.

For the United States, China is currently the second largest trading partner (after the EU), its third largest export market, and its biggest supplier of imports.

China's emergence as the world's second largest economy and the world's biggest merchandise exporter has been facilitated greatly by the openness of markets in the United States and Europe. As shown in Table 3, U.S. and EU trade deficits with China in recent years have been huge in absolute terms and they have also constituted a large share of each sides' merchandise deficits with the world. [36] At the same time, China's huge population and booming economy have made it a large, and one of the fastest growing markets for U.S. and EU exports and investment.

**Table 3. U.S. and EU-27 Trade Deficits with China, 2007-2009 (in U.S. dollars and % of U.S. and EU global trade deficits)**

| Country | 2007 | 2008 | 2009 |
|---|---|---|---|
| U.S. | -259 | -268 | -226 |
| % of U. S. global trade deficit | 32 | 33 | 45 |
| EU-27 | -221 | -247 | -184 |
| % of EU-27 global trade deficit/balance | 83 | 66 | 130 |

Source: Global Trade Atlas.

Notes: Trade deficits are for goods or merchandise only. The U. S. deficit with China in2010 was $273 billion, or 43% of the overall U. S. trade deficit. 2010 data for the EU are not yet available.

China's trade surpluses and use of interventionist and trade-distorting economic policies has contributed to growing trade friction with the United States and EU over a number of issues, including China's refusal to allow its currency to appreciate to market levels, its relatively poor record on enforcing intellectual property rights, and its extensive use of industrial policies and discriminatory government procurement policies to subsidize and protect domestic Chinese firms at the expense of foreign companies. These interventionist policies, according to both the United States and European Chambers of Commerce, have become more discriminatory towards foreign companies over the past several years, making it more difficult to export to China and to do business in China on a non-discriminatory basis. [37]

U.S. and EU trade officials have utilized two main approaches for addressing problems posed by Chinese policies and barriers that skew the playing field for trade and investment. The first has been to seek Chinese concessions during high-level summitry via the U.S. -China Strategic and Economic Dialogue (S&ED) and the Joint Commission on Commerce and Trade (JCCT) and, in the case of the EU, the EU-China High-Level Economic and Trade Dialogue. The second has been to bring disputes to the World Trade Organization, which China joined in 2001, when it is deemed that China does not comply with its WTO obligations. [38]

**Table 4. Current Account Positions of Selective Countries, 2008-2010 (in U.S. billions of dollars and Percent of GDP)**

| Country | 2008 | 2009 | 2010 |
|---|---|---|---|
| China ($) | 436 | 297 | 270 |
| China (% of GDP) | 9. 6 | 6. 0 | 4. 7 |
| Germany ($) | 246 | 163 | 200 |
| Germany (% of GDP) | 6. 7 | 4. 9 | 6. 1 |
| Japan ($) | 157 | 142 | 166 |
| Japan (% of GDP) | 3. 2 | 2. 8 | 3. 1 |
| United States ($) | -669 | -378 | -466 |
| United States (% of GDP) | -4. 7 | -2. 7 | -3. 2 |

Source: International Monetary Fund, World Economic Outlook Database, October 2010.

Notes: Data for 2010 are estimates.

Given the potential clout that China's two most important trading partners possess and the fact that the Chinese government does appear to respect economic strength, greater U.S.-EU cooperation arguably could increase the chances for successful outcomes through both dialogue and WTO litigation. Enhanced U.S.-EU consultation and agreement on common policy approaches to issues discussed in bilateral dialogues arguably could facilitate pragmatic solutions and more favorable results if China's leaders understood that there was a united front on issues of common U.S. and EU concerns. In the past, U.S. trade officials have often felt that their European counterparts have been less vocal in expressing concern and dissatisfaction with Chinese trade practices because they thought the United States would do the "heavy lifting" (i. e. , open the market) and they would then benefit from China's concessions. Understandably, given the very different experiences member states have in trading with China, the formulation of an EU-wide position is often difficult. From China's perspective, a fragmented, uncoordinated, and divided U.S.-EU approach may be preferable because it allows its policymakers to play one side off against the other, as it arguably did over the issue of currency manipulation at the 2010 G-20 meeting in Seoul.

In the case of WTO litigation, it seems that both the United States and the EU are increasingly willing to pursue WTO cases against China when it appears they are winnable. Cases where the United States and the EU serve as co-complainants arguably can enhance the profile of the case, but also ensure that China remains engaged and committed to the WTO dispute resolution process. While China initially settled many WTO cases filed against it before a panel was formed, since 2006 it has exhibited a new willingness to accept the decisions of WTO panels, thus encouraging a continuation of this approach when there appear to be clear violations of China's WTO commitments. In the process, China arguably could become increasingly vested in the maintenance of WTO norms and rules because it wants to be viewed as playing by the rules.[39]

Closer U.S.-EU cooperation in providing China with similar messages via high-level summitry or in filing WTO complaints, however, may not address numerous other trade and industrial policies that disadvantage U.S and European companies because they are too complex or fall outside the purview of WTO obligations, such as China's currency policy. In these cases, U.S. and European officials may still be able to cooperate on understanding and encouraging reformers in China to more actively support policies that will make China a more responsible stakeholder in the global trading system. [40]

## Reducing Global Imbalances

One of the underlying causes of the 2008 global recession was the presence of highly skewed trade imbalances driven by distorted global consumption and savings patterns. High savings countries like China and Germany produced more than they consumed and had to rely on export-led growth to keep their economies growing. As shown in Table 4, these two countries, plus Japan and some of the oil-exporting countries, experienced large current account surpluses in both the amounts and relative to the size of their economies. These surpluses, in turn, were recycled back to the United States, a low savings and large current account deficit country. The recycled funds, in turn, allowed the United States to finance a high consumption level, particularly in housing, that proved unsustainable.

Policies that correct the imbalances and provide for more balanced growth in the next decade are considered by many economists to be important for both global economic recovery and an avoidance of an outbreak of protectionism. According to this view, for large current account deficit countries like the United States, where domestic spending exceeds production, spending (both private and government) must decline and savings rise if the imbalances are to be significantly reduced. Because the U.S. adjustment involves going from the world's consumer and borrower of last resort to depending much more on export-led growth, large current account surplus countries like Germany and China will have to sustain their growth more by stimulating domestic demand and boosting imports and less by exports. This means that German and Chinese domestic spending will need to rise either through increases in consumption, investment, or government spending, or a combination of all three. [41]

At a November 2010 Summit in Seoul, leaders of the Group of 20 major economies (G-20) agreed to curb "persistently large imbalances" in trade that are deemed to pose serious risks to global economic growth and an open world trading system. While the group's communiqué reflected an emerging consensus that longstanding economic patterns – in particular the United States consuming too much and big trade surplus countries like China and Germany consuming too little – were no longer sustainable, agreement to monitor and address such imbalances in future meetings fell short of initial U.S. proposals to place quantitative limits on deficits and surpluses. [42]

China and Germany led the resistance to U.S. efforts to place limits on surplus countries. In the weeks prior to the summit, both countries countered U.S. proposals by criticizing the loosening of monetary policy (quantitative easing) by the Federal Reserve, arguably diverting U.S. pressure on them to reduce their surpluses. In the process, the G-20 Summit in Seoul revealed a new focus of conflict over the management of the global economy. While U.S.-China differences are the most prominent and longstanding, having centered on China's trade surpluses and its intervention in the foreign exchange market to keep the value of its currency from appreciating, the U.S. - German policy cleavage is newer and centered around macroeconomic policy disagreements. Reflecting perhaps a broader shift in European thinking, driven by German insistence on fiscal austerity, the new cleavage has the potential to challenge some of the underlying assumptions of the transatlantic economy and alter the international debate on global imbalances by positioning Germany and China against the United States on this particular issue. [43]

German policymakers reject the notion that the country's export surpluses need to be trimmed. German Finance Minister Wolfgang Schaeuble, for example, has argued that other countries, including the United States, should impose fiscal austerity and tighter monetary policy to right the global economy.[44] Due in part to the spillover effects of the Eurozone crisis (sovereign debt problems of Greece, Ireland, Portugal, and Spain), Germany has also urged its Eurozone partners (16 other members of the EU that share a common currency, the euro) to undertake austere economic policies.

Many German policymakers tend to believe that the Eurozone should be turned into a larger version of their nation – a zone where fiscal responsibility reigns and every country lives within its means. A Eurozone built on Germany's image, the argument goes, would be more prudent, responsible, and competitive. This view may be supported by many countries in northern Europe such as Austria and the Netherlands. A case can be made, in the midst of the Greek and Irish sovereign debt crises, that Eurozone members need to restore faith in the way they manage their public finances. However, if the current account surplus countries such as Germany and the Netherlands also pursue austere fiscal policies, the Eurozone may contribute little or nothing to global demand, thereby putting more pressure on the international trading system at a time when most countries around the world are trying to grow faster by exporting. [45]

One possible result of austere fiscal policies across the Eurozone, combined with the continuation of heavy German reliance on export-led growth, could be a weaker euro and slower growth across Europe. This, in turn, could lead to a big increase in Europe's trade and current account surplus with the rest of the world by several hundreds of billions of dollars. Coming on top of continuing Chinese and other Asian trading surpluses, European surpluses could help push U. S. trade deficits to record levels, risking an upsurge of protectionism. [46]

## OUTLOOK

U.S.-EU trade and economic relations are healthy, complex, and mutually advantageous. While the future of the relationship is difficult to predict, it appears unlikely that any new, major policy initiative will be advanced during the 112th Congress to accelerate the integration of the two economies or to foster greater government- to- government cooperation in dealing with mutual global economic challenges. The already high level of transatlantic market integration in goods, services, and capital may continue to be driven primarily by market forces.

Policy efforts to deepen U.S.-EU economic ties are likely to center around initiatives agreed at the December 2010 meeting of the TEC. As the TEC work program focuses on sectors where regulatory cooperation can help avoid the emergence of unintended trade barriers in emerging or new technologies, any future progress will affect a relatively small amount of trade. Whether the TEC will realize its potential as a mechanism to accelerate the integration of the transatlantic marketplace remains to be seen.

Greater collaboration in United States and EU approaches towards addressing global economic challenges remains a work in progress. While some convergence in approaches for completing the Doha Round and dealing with Chinese trade barriers appears to be taking place, the two sides remain far apart on how to reduce global imbalances. More active cooperation on issues where the two sides have shared interests may be impeded by a number of factors, including different priorities attached to the issues, competition between trade bureaucracies, and normal commercial rivalry between two economic superpowers for markets, jobs, and regional influence.

Different priorities may be the most important factor in keeping the two sides from advancing any major, new commercial initiative. The Obama Administration in its first two years was preoccupied with recession-related domestic legislation and health care. During this period, the President skipped attending a planned U.S.-EU Summit in May 2010, prompting assertions in Europe that U.S. interests were shifting increasingly to Asia and the Middle East.[47] The Obama Administration also procrastinated in hosting its first meeting of the TEC until December 2010, to the consternation of many EU trade officials. From the EU side, many of its top policymakers have been preoccupied with resolving the debt crisis in Greece and Ireland and related concerns about the stability and future of the Eurozone. In addition, EU trade officials now maintain that they have made more progress on regulatory and other non-tariff issues by negotiating free trade agreements with other countries than by entering into a regulatory dialogue with the United States.[48]

As U.S.-EU trade and economic interactions continue to play an important role in affecting growth and the creation of new jobs on both sides of the Atlantic, the 112$^{th}$ Congress can be expected to monitor ongoing efforts to deepen transatlantic ties. While political support for bold new undertakings may be lacking, U.S.-EU cooperation may continue to make incremental progress in addressing joint challenges.

## ACKNOWLEDGMENTS

Paul Belkin, William Cooper, Mary Irace, Derek Mix, and Wayne Morrison participated in the development of this report.

## End Notes

[1] The European Union is comprised of 27 member states: Austria, Belgium, Bulgaria, Cyprus, the Czech Republic, Denmark, Estonia, Finland, France, Greece, Hungary, Ireland, Italy, Latvia, Lithuania, Luxembourg, Malta, the Netherlands, Poland, Portugal, Romania, Slovakia, Slovenia, Spain, Sweden, and the United Kingdom. For background on the European Union, see CRS Report RS21372, *The European Union: Questions and Answers*, by Kristin Archick and Derek E. Mix.

[2] CRS Report RL30608, *EU-U. S. Economic Ties: Framework, Scope, and Magnitude*, by William H. Cooper.

[3] CRS Report R41411, *The Future of the Eurozone and U. S. Interests*, coordinated by Raymond J. Ahearn.

[4] CRS Report R41143, *Europe's Preferential Trade Agreements: Status, Content, and Implications*, by Raymond J. Ahearn.

[5] OECD Working Paper No. 432, *On the Benefits of Liberalizing Product Markets and Reducing Barriers to International Trade and Investment: The Case of the United States and European Union*, May 26, 2005.

[6] Stakeholder groups that have called for new approaches to reinvigorate transatlantic economic relations include the Atlantic Council, the Bertelsmann Foundation, the U. S. Chamber of Commerce, the Transatlantic Business Dialogue (TABD), the Confederation of European Business, and the European-American Business Council.

[7] CRS Report RL34717, *Transatlantic Regulatory Cooperation: Background and Analysis*, by Raymond J. Ahearn.

[8] Ecorys, *Non-Tariff Barriers in EU-US Trade and Investment: An Economic Analysis*, Report for the European Commission, 2009.

[9] For an account of these efforts, see CRS Report RL34717, *Transatlantic Regulatory Cooperation: Background and Analysis*, pp. 13-17.

[10] CRS Report RL34735, *Transatlantic Regulatory Cooperation: A Possible Role for Congress*, by Raymond J. Ahearn and Vincent Morelli.

[11] International Trade Reporter, "Transatlantic Council Meeting Advances Regulatory Cooperation, Innovative Strategies," 27 ITR 1963, December 23, 2010.

[12] See CRS Report RL34717, *Transatlantic Regulatory Cooperation: Background and Analysis*, pp. 7-9.

[13] The higher average tariffs for agriculture may reflect the strength of ongoing pressures to protect some farmers and products from international competition on both sides of the Atlantic. The data source on average tariffs is from various editions of the World Trade Organization's Trade Policy Review for both the United States and European Union.

[14] The Doha Round of multilateral trade negotiations, formally the Doha Development Agenda (DDA), is an ongoing attempt to lower trade barriers around the world. Commenced in November 2001 under the auspices of the World Trade Organization, the Doha Round is now the longest running multilateral trade negotiation in postwar history.

[15] These gains combine both short-run "static gains" and longer-run "dynamic gains. " Static effects are associated with an improvement in allocative efficiency as firms accrue cash flow benefits from elimination of tariff payments and intermediate and final consumers

benefit from lowerprices. Dynamic gains accrue after the elimination of tariffs has worked its way through the economy by triggering a reallocation of resources (labor and capital) and changes in the returns to the factors of production.

[16] These gains for both exports and GDP are assumed to occur by 2015, or five years after the hypothetical cuts are enacted.

[17] Fredrik Erixon, and Matthias Bauer, "A Transatlantic Zero Agreement: Estimating the Gains form Transatlantic Free Trade in Goods," European Centre for International Political Economy, ECIPE Occasional Paper, April, 2010.

[18] Free trade agreements can be consistent with Article XXIV of the General Agreement on Tariffs and Trade and now the WTO if they meet a three-part test relating to notification, trade coverage ("substantially all"), and level of barriers to third-country trade. However, the WTO, in practice, has not examined whether free trade agreements reported to it are consistent with Article XXIV.

[19] For example, in a multilateral context, proposals have been made to negotiate the elimination of tariffs for only a few selected sectors such as oilseeds and fruits and vegetables. Political sensitivities in restraining liberalization in sectors such as dairy and sugar remain strong.

[20] Fredrik Erixon and Gernot Pehnelt, "A New Trade Agenda for Transatlantic Economic Cooperation," *European Centre for International Political Economy,* Working Paper No. 09/2009.

[21] Dan Hamilton, *The Transatlantic Economy 2010: Annual Survey of Jobs, Trade, and Investment Between the United States and Europe,* The Center for Transatlantic, Johns Hopkins University, Brookings Press, 2010.

[22] Philip Whyte, "Narrowing the Atlantic: The Way Forward for EU-U. S. Trade and Investment," *Centre for European Reform*, April 2009.

[23] CRS Report RL33388, *The Committee on Foreign Investment in the United States (CFIUS)*, by James K. Jackson.

[24] European Commission, *U. S. Trade Barriers Annual Report,* 2008, p. 19.

[25] Office of the United States Trade Representative, *National Trade Estimates Report*, 2010.

[26] CRS Report RS21618, *The European Union's Reform Process: The Lisbon Treaty*, by Kristin Archick and Derek E. Mix.

[27] Member states have concluded some 1200 BITs, almost half of the BITs enforced around the world, to provide protection for fund repatriation and against unfair or uncompensated expropriation. They do not include market access or liberalization commitments. See Stephen Woolcock, *The Treaty of Lisbon and the European Union as an actor in international trade,* European Centre for International Political Economy, Working Paper No. 01/2010.

[28] Office of the United States Trade Representative, *Trade Estimates Report*, 2010.

[29] The Atlantic Council of the United States, *Transatlantic Leadership for a New Global Economy,* Policy Paper, 2007.

[30] Nicolas Veron, "Europe Needs Consistency in Welcoming Foreign Investors," *Bruegel,* January 2011.

[31] Jagdish Bhagwati and Peter Sutherland, *The Doha Round: Setting A Deadline, Defining A Final Deal,* High Level Trade Experts Group Interim Report, January 2011.

[32] According to USTR, under the current draft agreement, China would be allowed to exempt up to 420 industrial products from tariff cuts, India would offer no new market access for 97 percent of its total tariff lines covering industrial products, and Brazil would be shielded from increasing market access on nearly half of its industrial products. Nor have any of these three countries offered to provide significant liberalization of their services sectors. See Remarks by Ambassador Miriam Sapiro at the European Policy Centre, February 10, 2011. Found at http://ustr. gov.

[33] Gary Clyde Hufbauer, Jeffrey J. Schott, and Woan Foong Wong, *Figuring Out the Doha Round,* Peterson Institute for International Economics, June 2010.

[34] Statement of the U.S. Chamber of Commerce before the House Ways and Means Subcommittee on Trade Hearing, "Enhancing the U.S.-EU Trade Relationship," July 27, 2010.

[35] Ibid.

[36] The trade deficit with China has become a political issue in both the United States and the European Union. The underlying causes of these deficits are differences in savings and investment, and the shifting of production from many East Asian countries to China.

[37] CRS Report RL33536, *China-U. S. Trade Issues*, by Wayne M. Morrison.

[38] Charles W. Freeman III, "China's Trade and Industrial Policies," Testimony before the House Ways and Means Committee Hearing on *China's Trade Practices*, June 16, 2010.

[39] Marcia Don Harpaz, "Sense and Sensibilities of China and WTO Dispute Settlement," *Journal of World Trade Law,* December 2010.

[40] Charles W. Freeman III, "China's Trade and Industrial Policies," op. cit.

[41] An OECD analysis holds that Germany could best increase its consumption and living standards by opening its services sector to more domestic and international competition.

[42] Sewell Chan, "Obama Ends G-20 Summit With Criticism of China," *New York Times,* November 12, 2010.

[43] C. Fred Bergsten, "Worrisome Outcome from the G-20 Summit," edited transcript recorded November 12, 2010, Peterson Institute for International Economics Interviews on Current Topics.

[44] Cast differently, Germany is convinced that its current account surplus is the result of prudent economic policy and hard work and that it is not to blame for troubling global imbalances. But as a simple matter of accounting, a German or Chinese trade surplus must be offset by another country's trade deficit. In a recent interview, IMF Managing Director Dominique Strauss-Kahn observed that "you can't defend your own surplus and at the same time criticize others' deficits. "

[45] Philip Whyte, "Why Germany Is Not a Model for the Eurozone," *Centre for European Reform,* October 2010.

[46] C. Fred Bergsten, "A Return to Global Imbalances," edited transcript recorded June 15, 2010, Interviews on Current Topics, Peterson Institute for International Economics.

[47] CRS Report RS22163, *The United States and Europe: Current Issues*, by Derek E. Mix.

[48] European Commission, Staff Working Document, "Report on progress achieved on the Global Europe strategy, 2006-2010," Brussels, SEC (2010) 1268/2, p. 16.

# INDEX

## A



## B



## C

## D



## E

## P



## R



## S